The School of Christ

by

T. Austin-Sparks

Rickfords Hill Publishing Ltd.

Published by

RICKFORDS HILL PUBLISHING LTD.

P.O. Box 576, Aylesbury, HP22 6XX, UK.

www.rhpbooks.co.uk

First published 1942
This edition 2010

ISBN 978-1-905044-26-9

Scripture extracts are taken from the American Standard Version
unless otherwise noted.

Printed in Great Britain by Clays Ltd., St Ives plc.

Contents

Introduction

It was during a time of intense spiritual hunger that the ministry and writings of T. Austin-Sparks came to my attention. My dear friend Leonard Ravenhill asked me to read one of his most prized books. It was an out-of-print copy of *The School of Christ*. I was deeply moved by its liberating, refreshing, and spiritual message.

I believe the message and spirit of this book will profoundly affect any God-hungry servant of the Lord. Though Austin-Sparks is now with the heavenly Father, his dynamic messages are still changing the hearts of those who seek the deeper truths of the Spirit.

I agree with Brother Austin-Sparks that no man is of any use to God, in eternal values, if he has no settled assurance that he is accepted in the Beloved. Also, the true man of God must fully accept the fundamental principle that—*of himself he can do nothing, and all things are of and out of God.*

This is a book you will want to read many times. It was during my third reading that its truth fully dawned on me. It has affected my preaching, my outlook on life, and intensified my hunger for the glorious liberty of the Cross. We believe this book is destined by God to bless and edify numerous spiritually hungry ministers and laymen.

—David Wilkerson.

Preface to the Third and Revised Edition

The ministry contained in this little book has been wrought on the anvil of deep and drastic dealings of God with the vessel. It is not *only* doctrinal; it is experiential. Only those who really mean *business* with God will take the pains demanded to read it. For such, two words of advice may be helpful. Firstly, try to remember all through that the spoken form is retained. The messages were given in conference, and the reader must try to get into the spirit and mind of listening, and not only reading. In speaking, the messenger can see by the faces before him where repetition or re-emphasis or fuller elucidation is called for. This explains much that would not be the character of a precisely literary production. It has its difficulties for readers, but it also has its values.

Then, my advice is that not too much, indeed not a lot, should be attempted at once. Almost every page requires thinking about, and weariness can only overtake if too much is read without quiet meditation.

Of all the books that have issued from this ministry, I regard this one as that which goes most deeply to the roots and foundations of our life in Christ with God.

May He make the reading of it result in a fuller understanding of the meaning of Christ.

T. Austin-Sparks.

London,
July 1964.

1

The Foundation of Spiritual Education

Reading: Eze. 40:2-4; 43:10-11; Matt. 3:17; 11:25-30;
John 1:51; Luke 9:23; Eph. 4:20-21.

The basic word out of those read, for our present purpose,
is Matt. 11:29—*"Take my yoke upon you, and learn of
me."*

Learn of me. The Apostle Paul, in a slightly different
form of words, gives us what the Lord Jesus meant—*"Ye
did not so learn Christ"* (Eph. 4:20).

Leaving out one very little word makes all the
difference and gives the true sense. The Lord Jesus, while
He was here, could only put it in an objective way, for
the subjective time had not arrived: and so He had to say,
"Learn of me." When the subjective time came, the Holy
Spirit would lead the apostle to leave out the "of", and say
"learn Christ."

I am quite sure that many of you will immediately
discern that is just the flaw in a very great deal of popular
Christianity today—a kind of objective imitation of Jesus
which gets nowhere, rather than the subjective learning
Jesus which gets everywhere.

So for this little while we are to be occupied with the
School of Christ, into which school He brought the twelve,

whom He chose "that they might be with him and that he might send them forth" (Mark 3:14). They were first of all called disciples, which simply means they came under discipline. Before ever we can be apostles, that is, sent ones, we have to come under discipline, to be disciples, to be taught ones, and that in an inward way. It is into this school that every one who is born from above is brought, and it is very important that we should know the nature of it, what it is that we are going to learn, and the principles of our spiritual education.

The object of our schooling is first comprehensively presented

Coming into this school, the very first thing that the Holy Spirit, the great Teacher and Interpreter, does for us, if we are truly brought under His hand, is to show us in a comprehensive way what it is that we have to learn, to present to us the great object of our education. We read those passages in Ezekiel which I think have a great bearing upon this matter. In a day when the true expression of God's thought in the midst of his people had been lost and God's people were out of immediate touch with Divine thoughts, away in that far country, the Spirit of God laid His hand upon the prophet and took him in the Spirit in the visions of God back to Jerusalem, and set him upon a high mountain, and gave him that presentation of a new temple, forth from which would flow a river of life to the ends of the earth. Then He followed this up by going into the whole thing in the most minute detail, and later instructed the prophet to show the house to the house of Israel with a view to bringing about a recovery of spiritual life in conformity to that great comprehensive and detailed revelation of God's thought, that they should first of all be ashamed.

It is a much disputed matter whether the temple of Ezekiel will yet literally be set up on the earth. We will not argue about that, but of this one thing we need have no question, that all that Ezekiel saw has its spiritual counterpart and fulfillment in the Church which is His Body; spiritually it is all in Christ. And God's method with His people, in order to secure a full expression of His thought, is first of all to present the perfect Object: and this He did when at the Jordan He rent the heavens and said, *"This is my beloved Son in whom I am well pleased."* He presented and attested that which was the full, comprehensive and detailed expression of His thought for His people. The Apostle Paul, in words familiar to us, expressly voices the fact,

"Whom he foreknew, he also foreordained to be conformed to the image of his Son" (Rom. 8:29).

"This is my beloved Son in whom I am well pleased" —*"Conformed to the image of his Son."* There is the presentation and the attestation and the declaration of Divine purpose in relation to Him. Therefore I repeat, the Holy Spirit's first object is to acquaint us with what is, in view in our spiritual education; namely, that He is to reveal Christ in us and then afterward to get to work to, conform us to Christ. To learn Christ we must first see Christ.

The pre-eminent mark of a life governed by the Spirit

The mark of a life governed by the Holy Spirit is that such a life is continually and ever more and more occupied with Christ, that Christ is becoming greater and greater as time goes on. The effect of the Holy Spirit's work in us is to bring us to the shore of a mighty ocean which reaches far, far beyond our range, and concerning which we feel—Oh, the depths, the fullness, of Christ! If we live as long as ever man lived, we shall still be only on the fringe of this vast fullness that Christ is.

Now, that at once becomes a challenge to us before we go any further. These are not just words. This is not just rhetoric; this is truth. Let us ask our hearts at once, Is this true in our case? Is this the kind of life that we know? Are we coming to despair on this matter? That is to say, that we are glimpsing so much as signified by Christ that we know we are beaten, that we are out of our depth, and will never range all this. It is beyond us, far beyond us, and yet we are drawn on and ever on. Is that true in your experience? That is the mark of a life governed by the Holy Spirit. Christ becomes greater and greater as we go on. If that is true, well, that is the way of life. If ever you and I should come to a place where we think we know, we have it all, we have attained, and from that point things become static, we may take it that the Holy Spirit has ceased operations and that life has become stultified.

Let us take the example of one who is given to us, I believe, as amongst men, for this very purpose of showing forth God's ways, the Apostle Paul. The words which he uses to define and express what happened to him right at the commencement are these: "*It pleased God... to reveal his Son in me*" (Gal. 1:16). Now, that man did a very great deal of teaching and preaching. He put out a great deal. He had a long and very full life, not only in the amount that he put out, but in the concentrated essence which has defeated all the attempts to fathom. At the end of that long life, that full life, that man who said concerning its commencement, "It pleased God... to reveal his Son in me", is crying from his heart this cry, "that I may know him" (Phil. 3:10); indicating surely that with the great initial revelation and all the subsequent and continual unveilings, even being caught up into the third heaven and shown unspeakable things, with all that, at the end he knows nothing compared with what there is to be known. That I may know Him! That is the essence of a life governed by the Holy Spirit, and it is that which will deliver us from death, from stagnation, from coming to a standstill. It is the work of the Spirit in the School of Christ to present and to keep in view Christ in His greatness. So God, right at the beginning, brings Christ forth, presents Him, attests Him, and in effect says, This is that to which I will to conform you, to this image!

Yes, but then, having the presentation, the basic lessons begin. The Holy Spirit is not satisfied with just giving us a great presentation: He is going to begin real work in relation to that presentation, and we are, under His hand, brought to two or three basic things in our spiritual education.

The challenge and meaning of an open heaven

My aim, in co-operation with the Lord, is to make everything pre-eminently practical; and so we apply the challenge immediately, and I ask you, Is the Holy Spirit within you presenting God's fullness in His Son in an ever-growing way? Is that the nature of your spiritual life? If not, then you must have some definite exercise before the Lord about it; there is something wrong. The anointing means that, and if that is not the nature of your spiritual life, there is something wrong in your case in relation to the anointing. To Nathanael the Lord Jesus said, "Henceforth" (our old English word is "hereafter", but I think many people have mistakenly thought that means the "after life") "ye shall see the heaven opened, and the angels of God ascending and descending upon the Son of man." Hereafter, of course, was the immediate hereafter, the days of the Holy Spirit which were coming so soon. With an open heaven you see, and you see God's meaning concerning His Son.

That open heaven for the Lord Jesus was the anointing. The Spirit descended and lighted upon Him. It was the anointing, and it is the same for us. The open heaven is the anointing of the Spirit from the day of Pentecost onward upon Christ within us. That open heaven means a continually growing revelation of Christ.

Oh, let me urge this. I am brought back to urge this. We must not just add other things too soon, but make sure that we are right on these matters. The open heaven at once brings Gods revelation in Christ to your very door, makes it available to you, so that you are not dependent in the first place upon libraries, books, addresses or anything else. It is there for you. However much the Lord may see good to use these other things for your help and enrichment, you have your own open heaven, your own clear way through, and no closed dome over your head. The Lord Jesus is becoming more and ever more wonderful in your own heart, because "God, that said, Light shall shine out of darkness" hath "shined in our hearts, to give the light of the knowledge of the glory of God in the face of Jesus Christ" (2 Cor. 4:6).

The "other-ness" of Christ

That being true—and if it is not, perhaps you must just suspend things there until you have had dealings with the Lord—that being true, the Holy Spirit gets to work on that, as I said, to make two or three other things very real to us, the first of which is the altogether "other-ness" of Christ. How altogether other He is from ourselves. Taking the disciples who went into His school—it was not the School of the Holy Spirit in the same sense as ours is, but the result of their association with the Lord Jesus during those three or three and a half years was just the same—the first thing they learned was how other He was from themselves. They had to learn it. I do not think it came to them at the first moment. It was as they went on that they found themselves again and again clashing with His thoughts, His mind, His ways. They would urge Him to take a certain course, to do certain things, to go to certain places; they would seek to bring to bear upon Him their own judgments and their own feelings and their own ideas. But He would have none of it. At the marriage feast in Cana of Galilee, His own mother, with an idea, said, They have no wine. His reply was, "Woman, what have I to do with thee? mine hour is not yet come." What have I to do with thee? That is a weak translation. Far better, "Woman, you and I are thinking in different realms; we have at the moment nothing in common." Thus throughout their lives they sought to impinge upon Him with their mentality. No, all the time He was putting them back and showing them how different were His thoughts, His ways,

His ideas, His judgments; altogether different. In the end I expect they despaired. He might well have despaired of them had He not known that this was exactly what He was doing in them. Catch that and you have got something helpful. "Lord, why is it that I am always caught out, always making a blunder? Somehow or other, I always say and do the wrong thing, I am always on the wrong side! Somehow I never seem to come right in line with You; I despair of ever being right!" And the Lord says, "I am teaching you, that is all; deliberately, quite deliberately. That is exactly what I am bringing you to see. Until you learn that lesson, we shall get nowhere at all. When you have thoroughly learned that lesson, then we can begin constructive work, but at present it is necessary for you to come to the place where you recognize I am altogether other than you are. The difference is such that we move in two altogether opposite worlds."

This ordinary mind of man, at its best, is another mind. This will of man, at its best, is another will. You never do know what lies behind your motives until the Holy Ghost cleaves right down to the depths of your being and shows you. You may put your feelings and desires into the most devout terms. You may, like Peter, react to a Divine suggestion, "If I wash thee not, thou hast no part with me", and say, "Not my feet only, but also my hands and my head"; but it is only self coming up again—*my* blessing. I want the blessing, and so miss the whole point the Master is trying to teach. "I am trying to teach you self-emptying." He might have said, "and you are laying hold of every suggestion of mine for self-filling, to get; and I am trying to say, Give, let go!" This self comes up in the most spiritual (?) way. Self comes up for spiritual blessing. We do not know what lies behind. We have to come into a very severe school of the Spirit which eventuates in our coming to discover that our best intentions are defiled, our purest motives are unclean before those eyes; things that we intended to be for God, somewhere at their spring is self. We cannot produce from this nature anything acceptable to God. All that can ever come to God is in Christ alone, not in us. It never will, in this life, be in us as ours. It will always be the difference between Christ and ourselves. Though He be resident within us, He and He only is the object of the Divine good pleasure and satisfaction, and the one basic lesson you and I have to learn in this life, under the Holy Spirit's tuition and revelation and discipline, is that He is other than we are: and that "other-ness" is indeed an utter thing. That is one of the hard lessons.

It is certainly one that this world will refuse to learn. It will not have that. That runs directly counter to the whole system of the teaching of humanism—the wonderful thing that man is! Oh no, when you have come to your best, there is a gulf between you and the beginnings of Christ that cannot be bridged. If you attain *your* best, you have not commenced Christ. That is utter, but we perhaps hardly need that emphasis. Most of us have learned something.

But let us, while we know this in experience, take the comfort which comes perhaps from being told again exactly what is happening. What is the Lord doing, what is the Holy Spirit doing, with us? Well, as a basic thing, He is making us to know that we are one thing and Christ another. That is the most important lesson to learn, for there can be nothing constructive until we have learned it.

The first thing, therefore, is the altogether "other-ness" of Christ as over against ourselves.

The impossibility of reaching God's standard ourselves

Then, secondly, the Holy Spirit brings us face to face with the utter impossibility of our ever being that of ourselves. You see, God has set up a standard, God has presented His model, God has given us His object for our conformity and the next thing we come up against is the utter impossibility of being that. Yes, of ourselves it cannot be. Have you not learned that lesson of despair yet? Is it necessary for the Holy Spirit to make you despair again? Why not have one good despair and get it all over? Why despair every few days? Only because you are still hunting round for something somewhere, some rag of goodness in yourself that you can present to God that will please Him, satisfy Him and answer to His requirements. You will never find it. Settle it that "all our *righteousnesses* are as filthy rags." Our righteousness, all that trying to be so righteous, the Lord says of it all, "Filthy rags!" Let us settle this once for all. If you are looking ahead of what I am saying, you will see what it is leading to. It is leading to the most glorious position. It is leading to that glorious issue mentioned by the Lord Jesus in this way, in those days before things became inward: "Learn of me... and ye shall find rest unto your souls." That is the end. But we shall never find rest unto our souls until we have first of all learned the utter difference between Christ and ourselves, and then the utter impossibility of our ever being like Him by anything that we can find in ourselves, produce or do. It is not in us, in ourselves, in that way. So we had better despair our last despair with regard to ourselves. Those two things are basic.

A final word and exhortation

But then the next thing the Holy Spirit will do will be to begin to show us how it is accomplished. We are not going to start on that just now, but stay with the fact that the Holy Spirit can do nothing until these other things are settled. Oh, God is very jealous for His Son. His Son has gone right through the fires over this matter, having accepted man-form and a life of dependence, having voluntarily emptied Himself of that which meant that at any moment He could of Himself work by Deity for His own deliverance, salvation, provision, preservation; having emptied Himself of that right and said, I let go all My rights and prerogatives and powers of Deity for the time being and I accept man's position of utter dependence upon God as My Father; I meet all that man ever has to meet on man's level! (This does not mean that He emptied Himself of Deity, but of its rights *for the time being*.) He met it in every realm in its concentrated form and force and went through without a flaw as man for man, and went back to the throne on the merit of a complete triumph over every force that ever man has to encounter in satisfying God. Do you think that after that God is ever going to forgo His Son, and all that He wrought in man's behalf, and say, Only be at your best and that will satisfy Me? Oh, what blindness to Christ, to God, is this Christianity that is popular today! No, there is only One in this universe concerning whom God can say from His heart "in whom I am well pleased", and that is the Lord Jesus Christ. If ever you and I are going to come into that favour, it will be as "in Christ Jesus", never in ourselves.

When that is learned, or when that part of the education has been taken up, then it is that the Holy Spirit can begin the work of conformity to the image of God's Son. Well, we have seen lessons one and two in the case of the disciples. Through the months and years, they came to see how altogether different He was from themselves, and then came to the place of despair on that very matter as the Lord intended it should be. He foresaw it all. He could not hinder it, He could not save them, He had to allow them to go that way; and right at the end when they were making their loudest protestations about their loyalty, their faithfulness, their endurance, and what they were going to do when put to the test, He said to them all, "Do ye now believe? Behold, the hour cometh, yea, is come, that ye shall be scattered, every man to his own, and shall leave me alone" (John 16:31-32). And to one in particular He said, "The cock shall not crow till thou hast denied me thrice" (John 13:38). What do you think those men felt when He was crucified, and they had all run away, and left Him alone, and the one had denied Him? Do you not think dark despair entered into their souls, not only over their lost prospects and expectations, but despair over themselves. Yes, and He had to allow it. He could take no step to prevent it; it was necessary. And you and I will go the same way if we are in the same school. It is essential. No constructive work can be done until that has got advanced within us.

Well, that sounds terrible, but that ought to be encouraging! After all, it is all constructive in a way. What is the Lord doing with me? He is preparing a way for His

Son, He is clearing the ground for bringing in the fullness of Christ. That is what He is doing. He did it with them, and Pentecost and afterward was His answer to what happened on the day when He was delivered up, to all that happened with them. You say, Then He commenced His constructive work. Yes, He did; after the Cross and Pentecost, things began to change in an inward way, and from that time you begin to see that Christ is now manifested in a growing way in these men. They may have a long way to go, but you cannot fail to see that the foundation is laid, the commencement has been made. There is a difference, and the difference is not that they are necessarily changed men so much, as that Christ is now within them transcending what they are by nature. It is not that they become so much better, but it is that Christ within becomes so much more real as a power.

That is all for the moment. Let us bow our hearts today, yield today. It is the School of Christ. I know how challenging it is, challenging to this old man who dies very hard, yields with great difficulty. All our training, teaching, perhaps has been other than this. We have come into this horrible heritage of humanism—to be the best that I can be, to be my best! Well, you must take what I am saying in the sense in which I am saying it. No one is going to think that you can go and just be careless, slovenly, at your worst or less than your best, simply because of what I have said; but you know what I am talking about. At our best we can never pass across that gap between man and Jesus Christ. No, that gap remains, and the only way to get over is to die and to be raised from the dead; but that, for the moment, is another matter.

2

Learning the Truth

"Jesus therefore said to those Jews that had believed him, If ye abide in my word, then are ye truly my disciples, and ye shall know the truth, and the truth shall make you free. They answered unto him, We are Abraham's seed, and have never yet been in bondage to any man: how sayest thou, Ye shall be made free? Jesus answered them, Verily, verily, I say unto you, Every one that committeth sin is the bondservant of sin. And the bondservant abideth not in the house for ever: the son abideth for ever. If therefore the Son shall make you free, ye shall be free indeed" (John 8:31-36).

"Ye are of your father the devil, and the lusts of your father it is your will to do. He was a murderer from the beginning, and standeth not in the truth, because there is no truth in him. When he speaketh a lie, he speaketh of his own: for he is a liar, and the father thereof" (John 8: 44).

"Ye have not known him: but I know him; and if I should say, I know him not, I shall be like unto you, a liar: but I know him, and keep his word" (John 8: 55).

"Jesus saith unto him, I am the way, and the truth, and the life" (John 14:6).

"The Spirit of truth: whom the world cannot receive;

for it beholdeth him not, neither knoweth him: ye know him; for he abideth with you, and shall be in you" (John 14:17).

"But when the Comforter is come, whom I will send unto you from the Father, even the Spirit of truth, which proceedeth from the Father, he shall bear witness of me" (John 15:26).

"For the wrath of God is revealed from heaven against all ungodliness and unrighteousness of men, who hold down the truth in unrighteousness" (Rom. 1:18).

"For that they exchanged the truth of God for a lie" (Rom. 1:25).

"If so be that ye heard him, and were taught in him, even as truth is in Jesus" (Eph. 4:21).

"Put on the new man, which after God hath been created in righteousness and holiness of truth" (Eph. 4:24).

"These things saith he that is holy, he that is true" (Rev. 3:7).

"These things saith the Amen (=Verily), the faithful and true witness" (Rev. 3:14).

In our previous meditation, we were speaking together about the School of Christ, and we were saying that every true child of God is brought into the School of Christ under the hand of the Holy Spirit, the Spirit of the anointing, and that there the first great work of the Holy Spirit is to present Christ to the heart as God's object for all the Holy Spirit's dealings with us. Thus Christ is first of all presented and attested by God as the object of His pleasure, and then the Holy Spirit makes known the Divine purpose in connection with that inward revelation of the

Lord Jesus, namely, that we should be conformed to the image of God's Son. Then we were speaking about two or three basic lessons in the school, things which underlie our education. Firstly, the Holy Spirit takes pains to make all who are under this discipline (for that is the meaning of a disciple) to know in experience, in an inward way in their own hearts, the altogether "other-ness" of Christ from themselves. Then He also works to bring us to the place where we realize how impossible the situation is apart from miracles of God, that of ourselves we can never be like Christ. The one upshot of it all is that this must be something outside ourselves which is God's own doing.

Well, this is all preliminary in the School of Christ, although it seems to me that this preliminary education goes on to the end of our days. At any rate, it seems to be spread over a great deal of our life, though there should be a point reached which represents a definite crisis in the matter, at which a foundation is laid wherein these three things are recognized and accepted, and we shall not get very far until it is so. The person who really does begin to move is the person who has had his final despair over himself, and has come to see quite clearly by the Holy Spirit's illumination that it is "no longer I, but Christ"—
"Not what I am, O Lord, but what Thou art, that, that alone, can be my soul's true rest": Thy love, not mine; Thy peace, not mine; Thy rest, not mine; Thy everything, nothing of mine; Thyself! That is the essential foundation of spiritual growth, spiritual knowledge, spiritual education.

"I am the truth"

Now, in this meditation, we come to look at the Lord Jesus more closely as God's object and standard for the

Holy Spirit's work in us, this "other-ness" which He represents, and we have read a number of passages, all of which, as you noted, bear upon truth. Surely those passages in the Gospels must have played a part in the disciples' education. In the first place there was the statement or declaration made to the Jews—a tremendous thing to be said in the hearing of those disciples. There were Jews who made a profession of believing. The Lord Jesus raises the question of discipleship with them. He said to those Jews who had believed Him (it does not say they had believed *on* Him), "If ye abide in my word, then are ye truly my disciples; and ye shall know the truth, and the truth shall make you free." They answered back at once with the counter claim, "We are Abraham's seed, and have never yet been in bondage to any man." He presses this matter of the truth, truth in relation to Himself. "If therefore the Son shall make you free, ye shall be free indeed." "Ye shall know the truth, and the truth shall make you free." The question of whose seed they were arose, and associated with that the statement "if therefore the Son shall make you free, ye shall be free indeed." Do you follow that? Knowing the truth is knowing the Son. Freedom by the truth is by the knowledge of Him.

Then to the Jews—I presume of the more violent type—He said these words of unparalleled strength: "Ye are of your father the devil, and the lusts of your father it is your will to do. He was a murderer from the beginning, and standeth not in the truth... he is a liar, and the father thereof... when he speaketh a lie, he speaketh of his own." Tremendously strong language, and all on this question of the truth, the truth as bound up with Himself.

Then, when you come to chapter 14, He is with His disciples alone; and Philip says to Him, "Lord, show us the Father, and it sufficeth us." His reply is, "Have I been so long time with you, and dost thou not know me, Philip? he that hath seen me hath seen the Father." Another question in the school: "Lord, we know not whither thou goest; how know we the way?" "I am the way, and the truth...." I *am* the truth. The truth is not some *thing*; the truth is a Person. Well, all this is in the School of Christ, bearing upon Christ as the Truth.

I do not know how strongly you feel about the matter, but our object surely is that we should come to feel very strongly about these things. How do you feel about the importance of having a true foundation? And after all, the supreme feature in a foundation is truth, that the thing should be well and truly laid. This foundation has to take a fairly heavy responsibility, no less a responsibility than our eternal well-being and destiny, nay, the very vindication of God Himself. Therefore it must be absolutely true and the truth, and it surely behoves us to make very sure of where we are; in other words, to have done with all our unreality, to finish for ever with anything that is not genuine and utterly true in our position. It is just this that we are going to press and analyze for a little while now. So great are the consequences that we cannot afford to have anything doubtful in our position.

It is like this. You and I are going to face God sometime. We are going to come face to face with God literally in eternity and then the question is going to arise, Has God at any point failed us? Shall we be able, on any detail, to say, Lord, You failed me, You were not true to Your word? Such a position is unthinkable, that ever any being should be able to lay a charge like that at God's door, to have any question as to God's truth, reality, faithfulness. The Holy Spirit has been sent as the Spirit of truth to guide us into all the truth, so that there shall be no shadow whatever between God and ourselves as to His absolute faithfulness, His truth to Himself, and to all His word. The Holy Spirit has come for that. If that is true, then the Holy Spirit will deal with all disciples in the School of Christ to undercut everything that is not true, that is not genuine, to make every such disciple to stand upon a foundation which can abide before God in the day of His absolute and utter vindication.

The need for a true foundation

But in order that this may be so, you and I, under the Holy Spirit's teaching, have to be dealt with very faithfully, and have to come to the place where we are perfectly adjustable before God, where there is all responsiveness to the Holy Spirit, and nothing in us that resists or refuses the Holy Spirit, but where we are perfectly open and ready for the biggest consequence of the Holy Spirit putting His finger upon anything in our lives needing to be dealt with and adjusted. He is here for that.

The alternative to such a work of the Holy Spirit being allowed to be done in us is that we shall find ourselves in a false position, and it is far, far too costly to find ourselves in a false position, even though it only be on certain points. This is a false world we are living in, a world that is carried on upon lies. The whole constitution of this world is a lie, and it is in the very nature of man, though multitudes do not know it, but think they are true.

They are trying to build the world on a false foundation. The Kingdom of God is altogether other. It is built upon Jesus Christ, the Truth.

Well now, my emphasis at the moment is upon the need for a true position where we are concerned. Oh for men and women in whom the truth of Christ has been wrought and who will go on with God, no matter what it costs. "Who shall ascend into the hill of the Lord?" "He that speaketh truth in his heart... he that sweareth to his own hurt"—that is, who takes the position of verity though it cost him dear. We are influenced by all sorts of false considerations, influenced by what others will think and say, especially those in our religious circles, of our tradition; and they are false considerations and false influences. They bind and keep many men and women from going right on with God in the way of light. The issue is a false position at last.

Will you accept it when I say that there is no truth in us? This is one of the things we are going to find out under the Holy Spirit's dealings with us, that there is no truth in our minds naturally. We may be the most strongly convinced, and we may be prepared to lay down our lives for our convictions and to put everything into the crucible for what we believe with all our beings is right, is true, and in that very thing we may be utterly wrong. Such was the case with Saul of Tarsus—"I verily thought with myself, that I ought to do many things contrary to the name of Jesus of Nazareth" (Acts 26:9). Again, "The hour cometh, that whosoever killeth you shall think he offereth God service" (John 16:2); so zealous for their conviction— That is God's will! God's will!—convinced it is God's will; some to give their own lives on the strength of their conviction, and some to take other people's lives on the strength of their conviction. How far we will go on the strength of conviction and be wrong, utterly wrong, as utterly wrong as we are in earnest. A false conviction; and there is not one human mind incapable of getting into that state. The seeds of that are in human nature, in every one of us; in the mind as to conviction, the heart as to desire. We may think our desire is a perfectly pure and right one, and it may be utterly false; and so with our will, just the same. In us by nature there is no truth.

Living by the truth

I am going to get right down inside this thing. What is a Christian? A Christian is one who was not a very good tempered person, but is now good-tempered; not a very genial person, but is now very much more genial; a person who was not very zealous, but is now very zealous; a person who is different in disposition from what he was formerly. Is that a true definition of a Christian? Give me a homeopathic cabinet. Bring along to me a very irritable person. Give him a dose of, what shall I say?—nux vomica; in two or three hours he will be a very good-tempered man. Is he a Christian? Give him something else; turn him back to what he was before. Was he saved, and has he backslidden? Drugs can change a man's temper in a few hours. From being a lethargic, careless, indifferent person, you become alive, energetic, active; from being miserable, discontented, morose, melancholic, disagreeable, irritable, you become amiable, pleasant, relieved from all that nervous strain which was making you like that, and all that disordered digestion which was making you such a boor to live with. For a little while, you have made a Christian with drugs! You see the point.

Where is the truth? If the truth about my salvation lies in the realm of my feelings, my digestive system, my nervous organism, I am going to be a poor Christian; because that will be changing from day to day according to the weather or to something else. Oh no! Truth; where is the truth? "Not what I am, but what Thou art." That is where the truth is, "Ye shall know the truth, and the truth shall make you free." Free from what? Bondage! What bondage? Satan clapping his chains of condemnation upon you because today you are not feeling up to scratch. You are feeling bad in your constitution, and you are feeling depressed, you are feeling death all around, you are feeling irritable, and Satan comes along and says, You are not a Christian! A fine Christian you are! and you go down under it. Is that the truth? It is a lie! The only answer for deliverance and emancipation is, "It is not what I am, it is what He is; Christ abides the same." He is not as I am, varying here in this human life from hour to hour and day to day: He is other.

Forgive me being so strong in my emphasis, but I do feel this is the only way in which we are going to be saved really. Jesus, you see, says, "I am the truth." What is the truth? It is that which stands up to all arguments of Satan who is "a liar and the father of it." It is that which delivers us from this false self which we are; and we are a false self. We are a bundle of contradictions. We can never be sure that we are going to be of the same mind for long together, that our convictions are not going to do a right-about-turn. Oh no, it is not ourselves at all; it is Christ. You see what a false position we could be in if we were on that other level of nature. What a game the Devil could play with us.

I am using these illustrations to try to get to the heart of this. What is the truth? What is true? It is not found in us. We are not true in any part of our being. Christ alone is truth, and you and I have to learn how to live on Christ, and until we have done that the Holy Spirit cannot do the other thing. Perhaps you are saying, Is not a true Christian less ill-tempered? Is there no difference at all? Is a Christian right to be irritable and all that? I am not saying that, I am not letting you off on that; I am saying that in the school, until you and I have learned to hold on to Christ by faith, the Holy Spirit has not the ground upon which to work to bring us into conformity to Christ. If we are going to live upon the false basis of ourselves, the Holy Spirit leaves us alone. When we come to live by faith on Christ, then the Holy Spirit can come in and make Christ good in us, and teach us victory and teach us mastery, and teach us by deliverance how not to become a prey to good or bad feelings in ourselves, but to live on another level altogether. I mean this, that you cut the ground from under a great deal when you really get on to the ground of Christ.

Take irritability, for example. Some of you, of course, may never suffer in that way at all, but others do know what that battle is. Well, let us take such a case. Today we feel like that, all nervy, strained and short. What are we going to do about it? Are we going to make that our Christian life or the negation of our Christian life? If we come on to that ground, then Satan is always swift to make the most of it and bring us into terrible bondage and really to kill all spiritual life. But if you will take the position, "Yes, that is how I feel today, that is my infirmity today, but Lord Jesus, You are other than I am, and I just rest on You, hold on to You, make You my life", you see what you have done. You have cut the ground from under the feet of the Devil altogether, and you will find that there is peace along that line, and rest, and although you may still be feeling bad in the outer part of you, in the inner part you are at rest. The enemy is shut out from the inner part of you, he has no place there. The peace of God stands sentinel over heart and mind through Christ Jesus; the citadel is safe. What Satan is always trying to do is to get into the spirit through the body or soul and to capture the stronghold, the spirit, and bring it into bondage. But we can remain free inwardly when we are feeling very bad outwardly. That is freedom by the truth. That is the truth! Not a thing, not an affirmation, but a Person. It is what Christ is, and He is altogether different from what we are. Well, the Holy Spirit would teach us, as the Spirit of Truth, that it is abiding in Christ that means everything. The alternatives are to get into ourselves, or into other people, or into the world, in a mental way. Abide in Christ and there is rest, there is peace, there is deliverance.

But do not forget that, if we mean business with the Holy Spirit, He is not going to allow us to be deceived. I mean that the Holy Spirit is going to expose our true selves. He is going to uncover us and show us thoroughly there is nothing sound in us, nothing to be relied upon in us, in order that He may make it equally clear that it is only in Christ, God's Son, that there is security, and safety, and life.

I have a sense of failure in trying to convey to you what I have in my heart. So many people think that the spiritual life, the life of a child of God, is a matter of things. It is a thing called "the message of the Cross." It is a thing called "sanctification." It is a thing called "deliverance." It is thing called "death with Christ"—some *thing*. They are trying to get hold of it, and there is no deliverance that way at all. It does not work. "Its" do not work! It is all a matter of the Person, the Lord Jesus, and the Holy Spirit will never save us by an "it." He will always bring us to the Person, and make Christ the basis of our life, of our deliverance, of our everything. So the word is "Christ Jesus... is made unto us wisdom from God, both righteousness and sanctification, and redemption" (1 Cor. 1:30).

The abiding need of faith

Well, I must close. The work of the Holy Spirit is to conform us to Christ, to cause us to take the form of Christ, to form Christ in us; but Christ will always remain other than we are, so that there will never cease to be a call for faith. Do you expect to reach a point in this earthly pilgrimage when faith can be dispensed with? It is a false hope. Faith will be required as much as ever in your last moments in this life, if not more than at any other time. Faith is an abiding thing for the duration of this life. If that is true, that in itself dismisses any hope whatever of our having the thing in ourselves. That was the first sin of Adam, that choice of his, not to have everything in God, but to have it in himself in independence, to get rid of the idea of faith. So he sinned by unbelief, and all the sin that has come in since is traceable to that one thing—unbelief.

Faith is the great factor of redemption, of salvation, of sanctification, of glorification; everything is through faith. It undoes the work of the Devil. And faith simply means that we are put into the position where we have not got it in ourselves, we only have it in Another, and can only know it and enjoy it by faith in that Other. Thus Galatians 2:20 always comes with renewed force—"I have been crucified with Christ; and it is no longer I that live, but Christ liveth in me: and that life which I now live in the flesh I live in faith, the faith which is in the Son of God, who loved me, and gave himself up for me" (ARV). I live the life in the flesh by faith in the Son of God.

The Lord interpret His word to us.

3

Learning by Revelation

"In the visions of God brought he me into the land of Israel, and set me down upon a very high mountain, whereon was as it were the frame of a city on the south. And he brought me thither, and, behold, there was a man, whose appearance was like the appearance of brass, with a line of flax in his hand, and a measuring reed, and he stood in the gate. And the man said unto me, Son of man, behold with thine eyes, and hear with thine ears, and set thy heart upon all that I shall show thee, for, to the intent that I may show them unto thee, art thou brought hither: declare all that thou seest to the house of Israel" (Eze. 40:2-4).

"Thou, son of man, show the house to the house of Israel, that they may be ashamed of their iniquities, and let them measure the pattern. And if they be ashamed of all that they have done, make known unto them the form of the house, and the fashion thereof, and the egresses thereof, and the entrances thereof, and all the forms thereof, and all the laws thereof; and write it in their sight; that they may keep the whole form thereof, and all the ordinances thereof, and do them" (Eze. 43:10-11).

"In the beginning was the Word, and the Word was with God, and the Word was God. The same was in the

beginning with God. All things were made through him; and without him was not anything made that hath been made. In him was life, and the life was the light of men" (John 1:1-4).

"And the Word became flesh, and dwelt among us (and we beheld his glory, glory as of the only begotten from the Father), full of grace and truth" (John 1:14).

"And he saith unto him, Verily, verily, I say unto you, Ye shall see the heaven opened, and the angels of God ascending and descending upon the Son of man" (John 1:51).

God's answer to a state of declension

We have observed that, when the Divine thought as represented by the temple and Jerusalem was forsaken and lost and the glory had departed, Ezekiel was given and caused to write the vision of a new heavenly house, a house in every detail measured and defined from above. In the same way, when the Church of New Testament times had lost its purity and truth and power, and its heavenly character and order, and the primal glory of those early New Testament days was departing, then John was caused by the Spirit to bring into view the new, wonderful, heavenly, spiritual presentation, the person of the Lord Jesus; that new heavenly presentation of Christ which we have in John's Gospel, his letters, and the Revelation: and we must remember that the Gospel written by John is, in point of time, practically the last writing of the New Testament. Perhaps the real significance of this has not fallen upon us with due power and impressiveness. We take up the Gospels as we have them in the New Testament arrangement of books, and immediately we are

put by them back into the days of our Lord's life on the
earth, and from the standpoint of time that is where we are
when reading the Gospels. For us, all the rest of the New
Testament has yet to be when we are in the Gospels, both
as to the writings and the history which followed, all is
in prospect. That of course is almost inevitable, perhaps
almost unavoidable; but we must try to extricate ourselves
from that position.

Why was the Gospel of John written? Was it written just
as a record of the life of the Lord Jesus here on earth to go
alongside of two or three other records, that there might be
a history of the earthly life of the Lord Jesus preserved? Is
that it? That is practically the sole result for a great many.
The Gospels are read with a view to studying the life of
Jesus while He was on the earth. That may be very good,
but I do want to emphasize very strongly that this is not the
Holy Spirit's primary intention in inspiring the writing of
those Gospels. And this is particularly seen in the case of
John's Gospel, written so long after everything else, right
at the end of everything; for when John wrote his final
writings, the other apostles were in glory. John's Gospel
was written when the New Testament Church, as we have
said, had lost its original form and power and spiritual life,
its heavenly character and Divine order; written in the
midst of such conditions as are outlined in the messages
to the churches in Asia at the beginning of the Apocalypse,
and that can be so clearly inferred from his letters.

What was the object in view? Well, just this: as John
writes, things are not as they were, not as God meant them
to be; they no longer represent God's thought in and for
His people. The order, the heavenly order, has broken

down and is breaking down yet more. The heavenly nature has been forfeited and an earthly thing is taking shape in Christianity; the true life is being lost and the glory is departing. To that situation God reacts with a new presentation of His Son in a heavenly and spiritual way; for the features or characteristics of John are heavenliness and spirituality. Is that not true? Oh yes, here is a new bringing into view of His Son. But what a bringing into view! Not just and only as Jesus of Nazareth, but as the Son of Man, Son of God; God revealed and manifested in man, out from eternity with all the fullness of Divine essence, that His people might see.

So we must get to the Holy Spirit's standpoint in the Gospel by John, and in his other writings, and just see this, that God's way of recovery, when His full and original thought has been lost and that heavenly revelation has departed, and the heavenly glory has been withdrawn, is to bring His Son anew into view; not to bring you back to the technique of the Church or the Gospel or the doctrine, but to bring His Son into view, to bring Christ again in the tremendousness of His heavenly and spiritual meaning before the heart-eyes of His people. That is the answer that is found in John to these conditions that we meet with in the New Testament, which so plainly shows that the Church was losing its heavenly position, and all sorts of things were coming in, and the whole thing was becoming earthly. What will God do? In what way will He save His purpose which seems to be so dangerously near being lost? He will bring His Son into view again. Remember God's answer is always in His Son to every movement. Whether that movement be in the world as it heads up to

Antichrist (God's answer to Antichrist will be Christ in the full blaze of His Divine glory), or whether it be in the Church in declension and apostasy, God's answer will be in His Son.

That is the meaning of the opening words of the book of the Revelation. The Church has lost her place, the glory has departed, but God breaks in with a presentation of His Son.

"I am... the Living one, and I became dead, and behold, I am alive unto the ages of the ages, and I have the keys of death and of Hades" (Rev. 1:18 RV).

Christ is presented, and then everything is measured and judged in the light of that heavenly Man with the measuring reed in His hand. That is enough really, if we only saw that, and grasped it. Everything for God and for us is bound up with a heart-revelation of the Lord Jesus. Oh, it will not be, as I have said, in trying to recover the New Testament technique. It will not be in a restoration of New Testament order. It will not even be in the re-affirmation of New Testament truth and doctrine. These are things, and they can be used to form a framework, but they can never guarantee the life, the power, the glory. There are plenty here in this earth who have the New Testament doctrine and technique and order, but it is a cold, dead framework. The life, the glory, is not there; the rapture is not there. No, God's way of the glory is in His Son: God's way of the life is in His Son: God's way of the power is in His Son: God's way of the heavenly nature is in His Son. And that is John's Gospel in a few words, what God is there saying. It is all in the Son, and the need, the only need, is to see the Son, and if you see the Son by

God's act of opening the eyes, then the rest will follow. That is John's Gospel again.

"How opened he thine eyes?" Who did this? How did He do it? The man's response or reaction to the interrogation was this, in effect, You are asking me for the technique of things; I am not able to give you the technique, I am not able to explain this thing, but I have the reality, and that is the thing that matters. "One thing I know that, whereas I was blind, now I see." It is the light by the life. "In him was life and the life was the light...."

We do not want to be able just to give the technique of truth, and expound and define it all. That is not the first thing. The first thing is, the life produces the light and that is in the revelation of the Son: and if I must bring everything to a condensation it is this—firstly, God has shut up everything of Himself within His Son, and it is not possible now to know or have anything of God outside of the Lord Jesus, His Son. God has made this a settled thing; it is final, it is conclusive.

Christ known only by revelation

Secondly, it is not possible to have or know anything of all the fullness which God has shut up in His Son without the Holy Spirit's revelation of that in an inward way. It has to be a miracle wrought by the Holy Spirit within every man and woman if they are to know anything of what God has shut up in Christ. That again summarizes John's Gospel, for there at the centre is a man born blind. He never has seen. It is not a case of restoration with him, it is a giving of sight. It is the first thing. It is going to be an absolutely new world for that man. Whatever he may have surmised or guessed or imagined, or had described to him, actual seeing is going to be something with a new beginning. It is going to be an absolute miracle, producing an absolutely new world, and all his guesses of what that world contained and was like will prove to have been very inadequate when he actually sees. Nothing is going to be seen save by the miracle wrought within.

(1) God has shut up everything of Himself in His Son.

(2) No one can know anything of that save as it is revealed. "*No one knoweth the Son, save the Father, neither doth any know the Father, save the Son, and he to whomsoever the Son willeth to reveal him*" (Matt 11:27). Revelation can only come by choice of the Son.

Revelation bound up with practical situations

The third thing is this. God always keeps the revelation of Himself in Christ bound up with practical situations. I want you to get that. God always keeps the revelation of Himself in Christ bound up with practical situations. You and I can never get revelation other than in connection with some necessity. We cannot get it simply as a matter of information. That is information, that is not revelation. We cannot get it by studying. When the Lord gave the manna in the wilderness (type of Christ as the bread from heaven) He stipulated very strongly that not one fragment more than the day's need was to be gathered, and that if they went beyond the measure of immediate need, disease and death would break out and overtake them. The principle, the law, of the manna, is that God keeps revelation of Himself in Christ bound up with practical situations of necessity, and we are not going to have revelation as mere teaching, doctrine, interpretation, theory, or anything as a thing, which means that God is going to put you and me into situations where only the revelation of Christ can help us and save us.

You notice that the Apostles got their revelation for the Church in practical situations. They never met around a table to have a Round-Table Conference, to draw up a scheme of doctrine and practice for the churches. They went out into the business and came right up against the desperate situation, and in the situation which pressed them, oft-times to desperation, they had to get before God and get revelation. The New Testament is the most practical book, because it was born out of pressing situations. The Lord gave light for a situation. The revelation of Christ, we might say, in emergencies is the way to keep Christ alive, and the only way in which Christ really does live to His own. You understand what I mean.

Now then, that is why the Lord would keep us in situations which are acute, real. The Lord is against our getting out on theoretical lines with truth, out on technical lines. Oh, let us shun technique as a thing in itself and recognize this, that, although the New Testament has in it a technique, we cannot merely extract the technique and apply it. We have to come into New Testament situations to get a revelation of Christ to meet that situation. So that the Holy Spirit's way with us is to bring us into living, actual conditions and situations, and needs, in which only some fresh knowledge of the Lord Jesus can be our deliverance, our salvation, our life, and then to give us, not a revelation of truth, but a revelation of the Person, new knowledge of the Person, that we come to see Christ in some way that just meets our need. We are not drawing upon an "it", but upon a "Him."

He is the Word. "In the beginning was the Word",

and the meaning of that designation is just this, that God has made Himself intelligible to us in a Person, not in a book. God has not first of all written a book, although we have the Bible. God has written a Person. In one of his little booklets, Dr. A. B. Simpson has this illustration, or illustrates this thing in this way. He says that on one occasion he saw the Constitution of the United States written, and it was written on a parchment. He was near to it, and could read all the details of the Constitution of the United States. But as he stood back from that parchment, some yards off, all he could see was the head of George Washington there on the parchment. Then he drew near again and saw the Constitution was so written in light and shadow as to take the shape of the head of George Washington. That is it. God has written the revelation of Himself, but it is in the Person of His Son, the Headship of the Lord Jesus, and you cannot have the constitution of heaven, except in the Person, and the constitution of heaven is the Person in the shape of God's Son.

This is only an affirmation of things. I do trust you will take hold of the fact stated and go to the Lord with this. Do not ask for light as some thing; ask for a fuller knowledge of the Lord Jesus. That is the way, for that is the only living way to know Him: and remember God always keeps the knowledge of Himself in Christ bound up with practical situations. That cuts both ways. We have to be in the situation. The Holy Spirit will bring us, if we are in His hand, into the situation which will make necessary a new knowledge of the Lord. That is one side. The other side is that, if we are in a situation which is a very hard and a very difficult one, we are in the very position to ask for a revelation of the Lord.

4

The House of God

Reading: Ezekiel 40:2-4; 43:10-11.

You remember it was at the time when everything which had formerly been God's means of setting forth in type His thoughts in the midst of His people, had been broken down and lost, and the people were far out of touch both spiritually and literally with those things (the temple and Jerusalem, etc.), that the Lord took up His servant Ezekiel, and in the visions of God brought him back to the land, setting him upon a high mountain, and showed him in vision the city, and that great, new, spiritual heavenly house. Very full and very comprehensive and very detailed was the vision and the unveiling that was given, and the prophet was taken to every point, every angle, and through the whole of that spiritual temple step by step; in and out, up and through, and around, the angel with the measuring rod all the time giving the dimensions, the measurements of everything; a most exhaustive definition of this whole spiritual house. And then, further, after being shown all the form and the ordinances, the priesthood, the sacrifices and everything else, the prophet was commanded to show the house to the house of Israel and to give them all the detail of the Divine thought. In our previous meditation we pointed out, in that connection, that whenever there is a departure from Divine thoughts, whenever there is a loss of the original revelation of God, whenever the heavenliness, the spirituality, the Divine power of that which is of God ceases to operate in the midst of His people, and whenever the glory departs, the Lord's reaction to such a state of things is to bring His Son anew into view; and we followed through to see how that, in just such a time in the history of the Church in the first days, when things changed from the primal glory, John was used by the Holy Spirit through his Gospel, his Letters, and the Apocalypse, to bring the Lord Jesus in a full, heavenly, spiritual way anew into view; reminding ourselves, in so doing, that John's Gospel is practically the last New Testament book that was written, so that in spiritual value and significance, it stands really after everything else written in the New Testament. That is to say, it represents God's breaking in again with a fresh presentation of His Son in terms of heavenliness and spirituality, at a time when things have gone astray.

I just want for a few minutes, as I feel constrained, to stay with that: and we have the Gospel of John opened before us, at the first chapter. And note that this is God coming back in relation to the fullness of His thought for His people, and the meaning is just this: Christ is the fullness of God's thought for us, and the Holy Spirit (represented by the angel in Ezekiel), has come with the express object and purpose of giving and leading us into the detail of Christ, so that we get a comprehensive and detailed expression of the Divine thought in Christ and are brought thereinto.

Now you notice with John 1 you get the fresh, great, eternal presentation:

"In the beginning was the Word, and the Word was with God, and the Word was God."

That is the eternal background of Divine thought. Move on a little:

"And the Word became flesh, and tabernacled among us."

That is the Divine thought coming out of eternity and being planted right in the midst in a full and comprehensive way; all God's thoughts summed up in His Son, the great Eternal Thought, and centred in the midst of men in the Person of Christ. And then you move (and I am not touching all that lies between these points) to the end of that first chapter and you have by implication something that is very beautiful, if you recognize its significance. It is the word to Nathanael. It is always interesting to notice that it was to Nathanael. Had it been to Peter, James or John, we might well have concluded that it was for a sort of inner circle. But, being Nathanael, he is in the widest circle of association with Christ, and therefore what was said to him is said to every one.

"Ye shall see the heaven opened, and the angels of God ascending and descending upon the Son of man."

Bethel—the house of God

Now for the implication: we are instinctively carried by those words right back to the Old Testament, to the book of Genesis, and Jacob immediately comes into view, and we remember Jacob on his way between two points, as it were in an in-between place, between heaven and earth; neither wholly of the earth nor wholly of the heaven, but an in-between place. That night, in that in-between place, somewhere in the open he lay down and slept; and, behold, a ladder set up on the earth, the top of which reached unto heaven, and upon it the angels ascending and descending, and above the ladder the Lord; and the Lord spoke to him. And Jacob awaked out of his sleep, and said, Surely the Lord is in this place; and I knew it not; this is none other but the house of God! And he called the name of that place "Bethel", or the House of God.

The Lord Jesus appropriated that and made it to apply to Himself in His words to Nathanael, and, in effect or by implication, said, I am Bethel, the House of God; I am that which is not wholly of the earth, although resting on it; not wholly of heaven in My present capacity, though related to it; I am here between heaven and earth, the meeting place of God and man, the House of God, in Whom God speaks, in Whom God is revealed—He speaks in His House, He is revealed in His House—I am the House of God: the communications of God with this world are in Me, and in Me alone: "no one cometh to the Father but by me." He might well have said, although it is not recorded that He ever did so: the Father comes to no one but by Me.

Now, it is just that House of God, as represented by Christ, that is our thought as leading up to the practical testimony in baptism: Jesus—God's House. We know, of course, that every other house in the Bible is only an illustration of Him. Whether it be the tabernacle in the wilderness or the temple of Solomon, or any subsequent temple which was intended to fulfil the same function, or anything that in more spiritual terms in the New Testament is called the Church, it is not something other than Christ, but it is Christ. In the thought of God it is just Christ and there is nothing other than Christ and nothing extra to Christ which is the Church or the House of God.

The point that we feel the Lord is seeking to emphasize in these meditations is how He has bound up everything in a final way, conclusively and exclusively, with His Son, and that there is nothing to be had of God except in Christ, and by revelation of the Holy Spirit at that, as Christ is revealed by Him in our hearts. So that the Lord Jesus, being God's House, fulfils every function which is in type set forth in these other houses on this earth.

You begin with the Most Holy Place, the Holy of Holies. In Him is the Holy of Holies, where God verily and personally and actually dwells, has His habitation. God is in Christ, and in no other does He dwell in the same sense. It is going to become true that the Father will take up His abode in us. But, beloved, there is a difference. By the Father coming to dwell in us, we are not constituted so many more Christs. We are not in the same sense indwelt by very God as was the Son. The difference we will see in a minute. The indwelling of God in Christ is unique, and the Most Holy Place is in Him alone.

In Him is the oracle; that is, the voice, the voice that speaks with authority, and final authority. The final authority of God's voice is in Christ, and in Christ alone. The three disciples were in a very exalted position, both in their souls and in their bodies, on the Mount of Transfiguration. It was a wonderful, wonderful experience, a tremendous spiritual happening. But even so, when you are in a very exalted and elevated spiritual state, full of spiritual aspirations and spiritual expressions, you may make most grievous mistakes. So Peter, with the purest of motives, the highest intentions, said, "Lord, it is good for us to be here: if thou wilt, I will make here three tabernacles; one for thee, and one for Moses, and one for Elijah." And while he yet spake—as though God stepped in and did not give him a chance to finish, but said, Enough of that—while he yet spake, the cloud overshadowed, and there came a voice out of heaven saying, "This is my beloved Son, in whom I am well pleased; hear ye him." "Don't you begin to give expression to your thoughts and ideas here in this position: the final word of authority is in Him; you be silent to Him. Your spiritual ecstasies must have no place here; you must not be influenced by even your most exalted feelings." God's authoritative voice in Christ is the final word of authority. It is the oracle that is in Him, as in the sanctuary of old. So we may go through all of that tabernacle or temple and take it all point by point, and we see Him as the fulfillment of it all, as the House of God where God is found, and where God communicates.

The corporate house of God

Now, what is the House of God in its fullest sense, in its corporate or collective sense? It is, to take up that wonderful phrase with its almost two hundred occurrences in the New Testament, all that is meant by "in Christ." If we are in the House of God, we are only in the House of God because we are in Christ. To be in Christ is to be in the House of God, and not to be in Christ Jesus is to be outside of the House of God. He is the House of God. We are brought into Him.

But to be in Christ means a total exclusion of all that is not Christ, and in a previous meditation we strove to make one thing so clear, and that is, the altogether and absolute "other-ness" of Christ from ourselves, even at our best. How utterly different He is from man, even at man's religious best; different in mind, in heart, in will; different altogether in constitution, so that it takes us a whole lifetime, under the tuition of the Holy Spirit, to discover how different we are from Christ and how different He is from us. But God has ranged that difference absolutely from the beginning. It does not take God a lifetime to discover the difference. He knows it, and therefore He has put the absolute position from His own standpoint right at the beginning. He has, in effect, said, The difference between you and Christ is so utter and final that it is the width and the depth of a grave! It is nothing less than the fullness of death. There is no passing over. Death and the grave are the end. On the one side, therefore, is the utter end of what you are, and if there is to be anything afterward at all, that death must stand between, and anything subsequent can only be by resurrection: a passing out of yourself and into Him as through a death and a resurrection. So that, in that death, you are regarded as having passed out of the realm of what you are, even at your best, and as having passed into the realm of what He is. The depth of a grave lies between you and Him, and there is no passing over. It is an end. To get into the House of God means that.

The altar

Thus you notice, coming back to John 1, the truth is here set forth in a representative way. It is more fully and clearly developed later in the New Testament when the Holy Spirit has come for that purpose—He has come to take up what Christ has said and lead it out into its full meaning—but in John 1, long before you reach the House of God, you have this word reiterated, "Behold, the Lamb of God, which taketh away the sin of the world." Before you can get to the House, you have always to come to the altar. That is how it is in the tabernacle and temple. You can never get into the sanctuary, into the House actually until you have come to the altar. The lamb, God's lamb, and the altar, stand and bar your way to the sanctuary, and that lamb speaks of this dying in our stead, this passing out as us. We are identified firstly with Christ in His death, His death as our death. Then in virtue of His precious Blood which is sprinkled all the way from the altar right through to the Most Holy Place, in virtue of that precious Blood there is a way of life. It is His Blood, not ours; not our remedied life, not our improved life, not our life at all, but His. It is Christ and only Christ in the virtue of whose life we come into the presence of God. No High Priest dare come into the presence of God, save in the virtue of precious blood, the blood of the lamb, blood from the altar. Behold the Lamb of God! That stands right across the path to the House, the death in judgment, what we are. Well, these are hints from which you are seeing a great deal more, I expect, than I am able to say.

But what is particularly in view at this moment is this matter of being in Christ, and therefore being in God's House. The House of God is Christ, and if we speak of the House of God as being a corporate or collective thing in which we are, it is only because we are in Christ. Those who are in Christ are in the House of God, and are the House of God by their union with Him. They have come into the place where God is, and where God speaks; where God is known, and where the authority of God is in Christ absolutely, and we are carried in thought at once into Colossians, to Paul's word—"He is the head of the church." We see the Body and its Head. Christ's Headship means the authority of God vested in Him for government.

Baptism

Now you see two things. There is the first step toward the House, namely, the altar, the death, and that is what baptism is intended to set forth. It is that we take our place in Christ representing us, as the end of all that we are in ourselves. It is not only our sins that are taken away; it is ourselves, as so utterly different from Christ. *From God's standpoint*, it is an end of us. Let us understand that. That is God's standpoint. In the death of Christ, God has brought an end to us in our natural life. In Christ's resurrection and our union with Him, *from God's standpoint* it is no longer we who exist. It is only Christ who exists, and the Holy Spirit's work in the child of God is to make that which has been established in its finality real in us. We have not to die; we are dead. What we have to do is to accept our death. Failing to see that, we shall all the time be struggling to bring ourselves to death. It is a position taken which is God's settled, fixed and final position so far as we are concerned. That is the meaning of reckoning yourself dead. It is taking the place that God has appointed for us, stepping into it, and saying, I accept the position which God has fixed with regard to myself: the Holy Spirit's business is to deal with the rest, but I accept the end. If ever you and I should come to a place where we turn away from the Holy Spirit's dealings with us, what we are doing is something more than just refusing to go on. It is refusing to accept the original position, and that is very much more serious. It really is a reversing of a position which we once took with Him.

Well, now, baptism is that altar where God regards us as having died in Christ, and we simply step in there and say, That position which God has settled with reference to me is the one which I now accept, and I testify here in this way to the fact that I have accepted God's position for me, namely, that in the Cross I have been brought to an end. The Lord Jesus took this way and set baptism right at the beginning of His public life, and, under the anointing of the Spirit, from that moment He absolutely refused to listen to His own mind apart from God, to be in any way influenced by anything arising from the dictates of His own humanity, sinless as it was, apart from God. All the way along He was being governed by the Anointing; in what He said, what He did, what He refused to do; where He went, and when He went; and was putting back every other influence, whether coming from the disciples, or from the Devil, or from any other direction. His attitude was, Father, what do You think about this: what do You want: is this Your time? He was saying, in effect, all the time, Not My will, but Yours; not My judgments, but Yours; not My feelings, but what You feel about it! He had died, in effect, you see; He had been buried, in effect. His baptism had meant that for Him, and that is where we stand.

The laying on of hands

But then there is the other thing. When that position has been accepted in death, there is the rising. But, as

I have said, it is the rising in Christ, and from God's standpoint it is the rising, not only in Christ, but as under the Headship of Christ, or, in other words, under that full and final authority of God vested in Christ, so that Christ is our mind, Christ is our government, His Headship! And when believers in New Testament times had taken the first step in baptism, declaring their death in Christ, and had come up out of the waters, representative members of the Body, not always the apostles, laid their hands upon their heads and prayed over them, and the Holy Spirit signified that they were in the House. The Anointing which was upon Christ as Head now came upon them in Christ; not a separate anointing, but anointed in Christ (2 Cor. 1:21; 1 Cor. 12:13).

But what is the Anointing? What was the Anointing in the case of Christ, when He accepted a representative life and for the time being declined to live and act on the basis of Deity and Godhead, in order to work out man's redemption as Man? What did the Anointing mean? Well, in His case it is so clear. The Anointing meant that He was under the direct government of God in everything and had to refuse to refer or defer to His own judgments and feelings about anything. The Father, by the Anointing, was governing Him in everything, and He, apart from that, was altogether set aside. And when He said, "If any man would come after me, let him deny himself, and take up his cross daily, and follow me"; or again, "Whosoever doth not bear his own cross, and come after me, cannot be my disciple" (Luke 9:23; 14:27), He was only saying in other words, "You can never learn Me unless the Cross is operating continually to put you out and make way for Me, so that you can accept My mind, and the Cross means that you have to be crucified to your own mind about things: your mind has to come under the Cross; your will has to come under the Cross; your feelings and your ways have to come under the Cross daily, and that is how you make a way for learning Me, My mind, My government, My judgment, My everything. That is the school of discipleship, the school of Christ."

I was saying that, on the resurrection side, the Headship of Christ under the Anointing becomes, or should become the dominating factor in a believer's life, and the laying on of hands on the head is simply again a declaration that this one is under the Headship, this head comes under another Head, this head is subject to a greater Head. Thus far, this head has governed its life, but no longer shall this head govern its life; it is to be subject to another Headship. This one is brought under Christ as Head in the Anointing. And the Spirit attested that in the first days; the Spirit came upon them, declaring that this one is in the House where the Anointing is, to be under the government of the Head of the House.

The spirit of it all finds expression in that word in the Letter to the Hebrews, "But Christ as a son, over God's house; whose house are we" (3:6). I think it is unnecessary to say any more. We are just going on the way of the heavenly revelation of Christ; and, in baptism, we take the position of accepting God's position so far as we are concerned, namely, that this is an end of us! If in the future, what we are in ourselves seeks to assert itself, we should revert to this and say, "We said once for all—an end of us!" Preserve your attitude toward God's position.

Then afterward the gathering around and the laying on of the hands of representative members of the Body is a simple testimony to the fact that in Christ such as bear the testimony are in the House of God, under the government of Christ through the Anointing, and that His Headship constitutes us one in Him.

May the Lord make all this true in the case of all of us, a living reality, so that we really have come to Bethel and can say in our rejoicing in Christ, Surely the Lord is in this place! It is a great thing when we come to a spiritual position where we can say, The Lord is in this place. I am where the Lord is: this is the House of God! And that simply means a living knowledge of what it means to be in Christ, under His Headship and Anointing.

5

The Light of Life

"And, behold, the glory of the God of Israel came from the way of the east: and his voice was like the sound of many waters, and the earth shined with his glory. And the glory of Jehovah came into the house by the way of the gate whose prospect is toward the east. And the Spirit took me up, and brought me into the inner court, and, behold, the glory of Jehovah filled the house" (Eze. 43:2, 4-5).

"Then he brought me by the way of the north gate before the house; and I looked and, behold, the glory of Jehovah filled the house of Jehovah: and I fell upon my face" (Eze. 44:4).

"And he brought me back unto the door of the house, and, behold, waters issued out from under the threshold of the house eastward (for the forefront of the house was toward the east); and the waters came down from under, from the right side of the house, on the south of the altar" (Eze. 47:1).

"In him was life; and the life was the light of men" (John 1:4).

"Again therefore Jesus spake unto them, saying, I am the light of the world: he that followeth me shall not walk in the darkness, but shall have the light of life" (John 8:12).

"Jesus answered and said unto him, Verily, verily, I say unto thee, Except one be born from above, he cannot see the kingdom of God" (John 3:3, margin).

"When I am in the world, I am the light of the world" (John 9:5).

"Now there were certain Greeks among those who went up to worship at the feast: these therefore came to Philip, who was of Bethsaida of Galilee, and asked him, saying, Sir, we would see Jesus. Philip cometh and telleth Andrew: Andrew cometh, and Philip, and they tell Jesus. And Jesus answereth them saying, The hour is come, that the Son of man should be glorified. Verily, verily, I say unto you, Except a grain of wheat fall into the earth and die, it abideth by itself alone, but if it die, it beareth much fruit" (John 12:20-24).

"I am come a light into the world, that whosoever believeth on me may not abide in the darkness" (John 12:46).

"...in whom the god of this world hath blinded the minds of the unbelieving, that the light of the gospel of the glory of Christ, who is the image of God, should not dawn upon them" (2 Cor. 4:4).

"That the God of our Lord Jesus Christ, the Father of glory, may give unto you a spirit of wisdom and revelation in the knowledge of him; having the eyes of your heart enlightened, that ye may know what is the hope of his calling, what the riches of the glory of his inheritance in the saints, and what the exceeding greatness of his power to us-ward who believe, according to that working of the strength of his might" (Eph. 1:17-19).

The light of life! Before coming to a closer consideration of this matter of the light of life, may I just ask a simple but very direct question? Can we all say with truth of heart that we are really concerned to be in God's purpose; to know what that purpose is, and to be found in it? Everything depends upon whether we have such a concern. It is a practical matter. It should immediately swing us clear of just being interested in truth and increasing our knowledge or information about spiritual things. As we look into our own hearts at this moment—and let us do so, each one of us—can we really say that there is a genuine and strong desire to be in the purpose, the great eternal purpose of God? Are we prepared to commit ourselves to the Lord in relation to that in an utter transaction, by which we now have an understanding with Him that He will stand at nothing so far as we are concerned to secure us in His eternal purpose, whatever it may cost? As the Lord's people, are we ready to just pause and face that, and get right into line with God's end? I know that some of you are there, and that for you there is not much need of exercise about it, but it is quite likely that there are some who have taken things pretty much for granted. That is to say, they are Christians, they are believers, they belong to the Lord, they are saved, they put their faith in Christ, they have had association with Christian institutions and matters for so long, perhaps even from infancy. It is to such that I make this appeal at the outset. Here in God's Word that very phrase is used repeatedly—"according to his eternal purpose which he purposed in Christ Jesus before the world was." Is that the thing which stands foremost on our horizon or is it something remote, dim,

in the background? I press this, because we must have
something upon which to work. God must have something
upon which to work, and if that is the position, then we
can go on, and there will be a drawing out of revelation
as to that purpose and the way of it. But unless we are in
some quite positive position and attitude about it, you will
hear a lot of things said and they will simply be things
said, more or less of account to you.

The purpose of God

Well now, given that there is that concern, at least in
some measure, which justifies our going on, we ask, What
is the purpose of God? What is God's end? And I think
it can be put in one way amongst others. We can say that
God's purpose is that there shall come a time when He
has a vessel in which and through which His glory shines
forth to this universe. We see that intimated in the case of
new Jerusalem, coming down from God out of heaven,
having the glory of God, her light like unto a stone most
precious, as it were a jasper stone, clear as crystal. "Having
the glory of God!" That is the end which God has in view
for a people; to be, in a spiritual sense, to His universe
of spiritual intelligences what the sun is to this universe;
that the very nations shall walk in the light thereof, no
need of sun, no need of moon, for there is no night; and
that is only saying that God wills to have a people full of
light, "the light of the knowledge of the glory of God."
That is the end, and God begins to move toward that end
immediately a child of His is born from above; for that
very birth, a new birth from above, is the scattering of the
darkness and the breaking in of the light.

All along our way in the School of Christ, the Holy

Spirit is engaged upon this one thing, to lead us more and more into the light, "of the knowledge of the glory of God in the face of Jesus Christ", that it shall be true in our case that "the path of the just is as the shining light which shineth more and more unto the perfect day" (mid-day) (Prov. 4:18). Many people have thought—and, thinking so, have been disappointed—that that means it is going to get easier and easier, brighter and brighter, the more cheerful as we go on. But it does not work out that way. I do not see it to be true in the circumstances and outward condition of saints anywhere at any time. For them the path does not become brighter and brighter outwardly. But if we are really moving under the Spirit's government, we can say with the strongest affirmation, that in an inward way the light is growing. The path is growing brighter and brighter; we are seeing and seeing and seeing. That is God's purpose; until the time comes when there is no darkness at all, and no shadow at all, and no mist at all, but all is light, perfect light: we see not through a glass darkly, but face to face, we know even as we are known. That is God's purpose put in a certain way. Does that interest you? Are you concerned with that?

And that has a crisis and is also a process in spiritual life with a glorious climax in rapture. What I am especially concerned with now is the process.

We read in Ezekiel about the glory of the Lord coming and filling the House, and we have been seeing in previous meditations that the Lord Jesus is that House. He is the great Bethel of God on whom the angels ascend and descend, in whom God is found, in whom God speaks (the place of the oracle), in whom is the Divine authority, the final word. He is the House, and the glory of the Lord is in Him, the light of God is in Him.

The place of the shekinah glory

Looking backward at that tabernacle or that temple of old where the Shekinah glory was found, we mark that that light, that glory which linked heaven and earth like a ladder, had its expression in the Most Holy Place. You know that in the Holy of Holies, everything was curtained around and over, excluding every bit of natural light, so that the place, entered into apart from the Shekinah, would have been black darkness, without light at all; but entered into while the glory rested upon it, it was all light, it was all Divine light, heavenly light, the light of God. And that Most Holy Place sets forth the inner life of the Lord Jesus, His spirit where God is found, the light from heaven, the light of what God is in Him. His spirit is the Most Holy Place, in the holy House of God, and it was there, in that Most Holy Place where the light of the glory was, that God said He would commune with His people through their representative. "I will commune with you above the mercy seat between the cherubim" (Exo. 25:22). The place of communion—"I will commune." What a lovely word—"commune." There is nothing hard, nothing terrible, nothing fearful about that. "I will commune with you." It is the place where God speaks; in the communion God speaks, makes Himself known. It is the place of speaking. It is called the place of the oracle, the place of the speaking; and that is the Propitiatory, the Mercy Seat, and that is all the Lord Jesus. He, we are told, has been set forth by God to be a propitiatory (Rom. 3:25), and in Him

God communes with His people. In Him God speaks to and with His people.

But the underlining must be of those words "*in Him*", for there is no communion with God, no communion of God, no speaking to be heard, no meeting at all, save in Christ. That would be a place of death and destruction for the natural man; hence the terrible warnings given about coming into that place without the right equipment, that symbolic equipment which spoke of the natural man having been altogether covered and another heavenly Man having enfolded him as with heavenly robes, the robes of righteousness. Only so dare he enter into that place: otherwise it was "lest he die...."

If you want to know exactly how that works out, come over to the New Testament and take up the story of the journey of Saul of Tarsus to Damascus. He says, "At midday, O king, I saw on the way a light from heaven, above the brightness of the sun... And when we were all fallen to the earth, I heard a voice saying unto me... Saul, Saul, why persecutest thou me?" Then you will remember how they lifted him up and led him into the city, because he was without sight. By the mercy of God, he was without sight only for three days and three nights. God commissioned Ananias to go and visit that blinded man, and say to him, "Jesus, who appeared unto thee in the way which thou camest, hath sent me, that thou mayest receive thy sight." Saul of Tarsus would otherwise have been a blind man to the end of his life. That is the effect of a natural man encountering the glory of God in the face of Jesus Christ. It is destruction. There is no place for the natural man in the presence of that light; it would be death. But in John 8 we have those words, "the light of *life*", over against the darkness of death. Well, in Jesus Christ the natural man is regarded as having been entirely put away. There is no place for him there.

No place for the natural man

That means that the natural man cannot come into the light, nor can he come into God's great purpose and be found in that House full of His glory, that vessel through which He is going to manifest that glory to His universe. The natural man cannot come in there: and when we speak about the natural man, we are not just referring to the unsaved man, that is, the man who has never come to the Lord Jesus. We are speaking about the man whom God has reckoned as being put aside altogether.

The Apostle Paul had to speak to Corinthian believers along these lines. They were converted people, saved people, but they were enamoured of this world's wisdom and this world's power; that is, of natural wisdom, knowledge, and the strength that comes by it, and their disposition or inclination was to try to seek to take hold of Divine things and analyze them and investigate them, and probe into them along the lines of natural wisdom and understanding, philosophy, the philosophy and wisdom of this world. So they were bringing the natural man to bear upon Divine things, and the Apostle wrote to them, and in their own language he said, "Now the man of soul" (not the unregenerate man, not the man who has never had a transaction with the Lord Jesus on the basis of His atoning work for salvation; no, not that man) "the man of soul receiveth not the things of the Spirit of God, neither can he know them" (I Cor. 2:14). The man of the *psuche* [gr. *soul*], that is the natural man. The newest of our sciences is psychology, the science of the soul: and what is psychology? It has to do with the mind of man; it is the science of man's mind; and here is the word now—I am paraphrasing this because this is exactly what it means—Now the science of the mind can never receive the things of the Spirit of God, neither can it know them. This man is very clever, very intellectual, very highly trained, with all his natural senses brought to a high state of development and acuteness, yet this man is outside when it comes to knowing the things of God: he cannot, he is outside. For the first glimmer of the knowledge of God a miracle has to be wrought, by which blind eyes which never have seen are given sight, and by which light comes as by a flash of revelation, so that it can be said, "Blessed art thou... for flesh and blood hath not revealed it unto thee, but my Father which is in heaven."

This is stating a tremendous fact. Every bit of real light which is in the direction of that ultimate effulgence, the revealing of the glory of God in us and through us, every bit of it is in Christ Jesus, and can only be had in Him on the basis of the natural man having been altogether put outside, put away, and a new man having been brought into being with a new set of spiritual faculties: so that Nicodemus, the best product of the religious school of his day and of his world, is told, "Except one be born anew (or from above), he cannot see...." He cannot see. Well, it resolves itself into this, that to know even the first letters of the Divine alphabet we must be in Christ, and every bit that follows is a matter of learning Christ, knowing what it means to be in Christ.

How we get the light of life

(a) The crisis

That brings us to this question. What is the way into Christ, or how do we get the light of life? Well, the answer is, of course, briefly, to have the light we have to have the life. This light is the light of life. It is the product of life. All Divine light, true light from God, is living light. It is never theoretical light, mere doctrinal light, it is living light. And how do we get this light of life?

We have these two things brought very much before us in this Gospel of John, namely, Christ in us, and we in Christ. The Lord has given us a beautiful illustration of what that means, and that illustration we have read in chapter 12. What is it to be in Christ? What is it to have Christ in us? What is it to be in the life and in the light? What is it to have the life and the light in us? Well, here it is. There is life in that grain of wheat, but it is just one single grain. I want to get the life that is in that single grain into a whole host of grains, enough grains to cover the earth. How shall I do it? Well, the Lord says, put it into the ground: let it fall into the earth and die; let it fall into the dark earth, and let the earth cover it over. What happens? It immediately begins to disintegrate, to fall apart, to yield itself up, as to its own individual and personal life alone. Presently a shoot begins to break through the earth and up the stalk comes, and eventually there is an ear, a heavy ear, of grains of wheat; and if I could actually see life and look into those grains of wheat, I should see that life which was in the one in every one of them. Then I sow that ear, be it one hundred grains I sow, and I get ten thousand; and I sow them again, and they are multiplied a hundredfold, and so on until the earth is full; and if I could look with a magnifying glass into every one of those millions and millions of grains, and life was something visible to the eye, I should see that that same original life was the life of every one of them. That is the answer.

How does this life get into us, this light of life? The Lord Jesus says that death must take place, a death to what we are in ourselves, a death to our own life, a death to a life apart from Him. We must go down with Him into death, and there, under the act of the Spirit of God in union with Christ buried, there is a transmission of His life to us, and He, coming up no longer merely as a single grain of wheat, comes up manifold in every one of us. It is the miracle that is going on every year in the natural realm, and it is just exactly the principle by which the Lord gets into us. You see the necessity of our ceasing to have a life apart from the Lord, the necessity of our letting that life of ours go absolutely. That is a crisis at the beginning, a real crisis. Sooner or later, it has to be a crisis.

Some may say, I have not had that crisis. For me becoming a Christian was a very, very simple thing. As a child, I was simply taught, or, At sometime I simply expressed my personal faith in the Lord Jesus in some way, and from that time I belonged to the Lord; I am a Christian! Are you moving on in the growing fullness of the revelation of the Lord Jesus? Are you? Have you an open heaven? Is God in Christ revealing Himself to you in ever greater wonder and fullness? Is He? I am not saying that you do not belong to the Lord Jesus, but I am saying to you that the unalterable basis of an open heaven is a grave, and a crisis at which you come to an end of your own self-

life. It is the crisis of real experimental identification with
Christ in His death, not now for your sins, but as you.
Your open heaven depends upon that. It is a crisis. And so
with not one or two but with many this has been the way.
The truth is this, that they were the Lord's children; they
knew Christ, they were saved, they had no doubt about
that; but then the time came when the Lord, the Light of
Life, showed to them that He not only died to bear their
sins in His body on the tree, but He Himself represented
them in the totality of their natural life, to put it aside. It
was the man, and not only his sins, that went to the Cross.
That man is you, that man is me: and many, after years of
being Christians, have come to that tremendous crisis of
identification with Christ as men, as women, as a part of
the human race; not only as sinners, but as a part of a race;
natural men, not unregenerate, but natural men, all that
we are in our natural life. Many have come to that crisis,
and from that time everything has been on a vast, a vaster
scale than ever before in the Christian life. There has been
the open heaven, the enlarged vision, the light of life in a
far greater way.

   How does it come about? Just like that, and that crisis is
a crisis for us all. If you have not had that crisis, you ask
the Lord about it. Mark you, if you are going to have that
transaction with the Lord, you are asking for something,
you are asking for trouble; for, as I said before, this
natural man dies hard; he clings tenaciously, he does not
like being put aside. Look at that grain of wheat. When it
has fallen into the ground, look at what happens to it. Do
you think it is pleasant? What is happening? It is losing
its own identity. You cannot recognize it. Take it out and

have a look at it. Is this that lovely little grain of wheat I put into the ground? What an ugly thing it has become! It has lost all its own identity, lost its own cohesiveness; it is all falling to pieces. How ugly! Yes, that is what death does. This death of Christ as it is wrought in us breaks up our own natural life. It scatters it, pulls it to pieces, takes all its beauty away. We begin to discover that, after all, there is nothing in us but corruption. That is the truth. Falling apart, we are losing all that beauty that was there from the natural point of view, perhaps, as men saw it. It is no pleasant thing to fall into the ground and die. That is what happens.

"But if it die...." "If we died with Christ, we believe that we shall also live with him" (Rom. 6:8). We shall share His life, take another life, and then a new form is given, a new life; not ours, but His. It is a crisis. I do urge upon you to have real dealings with the Lord about this matter. But if you do, expect what I have said, expect that you are going to fall to pieces, expect that the beauty you thought was there will be altogether marred; expect to discover that you are far more corrupt than ever you thought you were; expect that the Lord will bring you to a place where you cry, Woe is me for I am undone! But then the blessing that will come will just be this—O Lord, the best thing that can happen for me is that I shall die! And the Lord will say, That is exactly what I have been working at, I cannot glorify that corruption. "This corruptible must put on incorruption" (1 Cor. 15:53), and that incorruption is the germ of that Divine life in the seed which yields its own life up, that is transmitted from Him. God is not going to glorify this humanity. He is going to make us like

Christ's glorious body. That is far too deep, and too much ahead, but our point is that there has to be this crisis if we are coming to the glory, God's end.

(b) The process

Then there is going to be a process. The Lord Jesus said, "If any man would come after me, let him deny himself, and take up his cross daily, and follow me", and in so saying He stated the basic principle. That the Cross is something taken up or entered into once for all is true, as to the crisis in which we say, Lord I accept once for all what the Cross means! But we are going to find that after the crisis, the all-inclusive crisis, day by day the Cross has to be adhered to, and the Cross is working out in those afflictions and sufferings which the Lord is allowing to come upon His people. He has put you in a difficult situation in His sovereignty; a difficult home, business, physical situation, a difficult situation with some relation. Beloved, that is the outworking of the Cross in your experience, in order to make a way for the Lord Jesus to have a larger place. It is going to make a way for His patience, the endurance of Christ, for the love of Christ. It is going to make a way for Him: and you have not to go to your knees every morning and say, Oh, Lord, get me out of this home, get me out of this business, get me out of this difficulty! You are to say, Lord, if this is the Cross in its expression for me today, I take it up today. Facing the situation like that, you will find there is strength, there is victory, the co-operation of the Lord, and there is fruit and not barrenness. It is in that sense that the Lord stated the basic principle in making the Cross a daily experience. "Whosoever doth not bear his own cross, and come after me, cannot be my disciple"—one of My taught ones, one learning Me! So that the taking up of this difficulty, whatever it be, day by day, is the very way in which I am learning Christ, and it is the process of light, the light of life, coming to know, coming to see, coming into fullness. You and I can never see and know apart from the Cross. The Cross has to clear the ground of this natural life. The Lord knows what we would do if He lifted away the Cross from us every day. I wonder what we would do.

It may not be just the later New Testament phraseology, or way of putting it, to speak of our daily cross, bearing my cross daily. The principle may more truly be that it is the Cross which is given to Him and becomes mine daily. That may be true, but it just works out this way. If the Lord lifted that which is the expression of the Cross for us day by day and took it off our shoulders, it would not be for our good. It would at once clear the way for the uprising of the natural life. You can see when people begin to get a bit of relief from trial. How they throw their weight about! They get on stilts, they are looking down on you; you are wrong, they are right. Pride, self-sufficiency, all comes up. Well, then, what about Paul? I look up to Paul as a giant, spiritually. Beside that man we are puppets spiritually, and yet, Paul, spiritual giant that he was, humbly confessed that the Lord sent him a messenger of Satan to buffet him, a stake through his flesh, lest he should be exalted above measure. Yes, spiritual giants can exalt themselves if the Lord does not see to it and take precautions, and in order to keep the way of that great revelation opened and clear, that it might grow and grow, the Lord said, "Paul, I must keep you down very low, very much under limitation; it is the only way: immediately you begin to get up, Paul, you are going to limit the light, spoil the revelation."

Well, there is the principle. The light of life. It is His life: and so again the Apostle says,

"Always bearing about in the body the dying of Jesus, *that the life also of Jesus* may be manifested in our body" (2 Cor. 4:10).

His life is what we need, and with the life comes the light. It is light by life. There is no other real Divine light, only that which comes out of His life within us, and it is His death wrought in us that clears the way for His life.

I must close there. See again God's end; light, glory, the fullness coming in. It is in Christ. The measure of the light, the measure of the glory, is going to be the measure of Christ, and the measure of Christ is going to depend entirely upon what space the Lord can find for Himself in us; and, for space to be made for Him, we must come to the place where the utterness of the setting aside of the self-life has been accomplished: and that takes a whole lifetime. But, blessed be God, there is the glorious climax, when He shall come to be glorified in His saints and to be marvelled at in all them that believe. Marvelled at! Having the glory of God! Oh, may something of the light of that glory fall upon our hearts now to encourage and comfort us in the way, to strengthen our hearts to go on in the knowledge of His Son, for His Name's sake.

6

An Open Heaven

We have been led to think in these meditations about being in the School of Christ, where all the learning, all the instruction, all the discipline, is toward knowing Christ, learning Christ; not learning about Christ, but learning Christ. That is the point of greatest difficulty in trying to make things plain and clear. We could take up everything there is about Christ as doctrine, as teaching, but that is not what we are after. That is not what the Lord is after at all. It is Christ Himself. He Himself is the living, personal embodiment, the personification of all truth, of all life, and the Lord's purpose and will for us is not to come to know truth in its manifold aspects, but to know the Person, the living Person in a living way, and that the Person being imparted to us, and we being incorporated into the Person, all the truth becomes living truth rather than merely theoretical or technical truth.

Just a word of repetition here: and I cannot tell you with what force this has come to my own heart and how heavily it rests upon me in its meaning. Whenever things are in danger of departing from His full, His complete, thought, God will always seek to bring back a fresh revelation of His Son. He will not lead to the recapture of truths as such. He will bring back all that is necessary by a fresh revelation of His Son, an unveiling or presentation of His Son in fullness. In that connection we have more than once said in these meditations that the Gospel written by John and his Letters and the Apocalypse, are the final things of the New Testament dispensation. They were written and brought in when the New Testament Church was departing from its primal and pristine glory, and purity, and truth, and holiness, and spirituality, and becoming an earthly Christian system. The Lord's way of meeting that situation was through these writings which are a new presentation of His Son in heavenly, Divine, spiritual fullness. It is a coming back to Christ, and the Holy Spirit would do that all the time. He would bring us back to the Person, to show us what that Person represents in a spiritual and heavenly way. We must be very careful that in our passing on from the Gospels to the Epistles, we do not get even unconsciously into the position that we have left elementary things and gone on to something that is not so elementary; that is, that the Epistles are something very much in advance of the Gospels. Emphatically they are not. They are only the opening up of the Gospels. All that is in the Epistles is there in the Gospels, but the Epistles are simply the interpretation of Christ, and the Lord would never have us occupied with the interpretation to the loss of the Person.

All things in Christ

Now, if I were talking to people who were responsible in the matter of Church building, that would be a very profitable matter with which to stay for a little while; but it just amounts to this for us. We take the Acts and the Epistles as setting forth the technique of the Church and churches and adopt it as a crystallized system of practice, order, form, teaching, and the weakness in the whole position is just this, that that is something as in itself, and the Lord Jesus has been missed and lost. I wonder if you detect what I mean by that? You see, the Holy Spirit's way is to take Christ and open up Christ to the heart, and show that Christ is a heavenly order; not that the Epistles set forth as a manual a heavenly order, but that Christ is that order, and everything in the matter of order has to be kept immediately in relation to the living Person. If it becomes some *thing*, then it becomes an earthly system; and you can make out of the Epistles a hundred different earthly systems all built upon the Epistles. They will be made to support any number of different systems, different interpretations, represented by Christian orders here, and the reason is that they have been divorced from the Person.

You see there are numerous things, numerous subjects, themes, teachings. There is the "kingdom of God", there is "sanctification", there is "eternal life", there is "the victorious life", "the overcomer" or "the overcoming life", there is "the second coming of Christ." These are but a few subjects, themes, truths, as they are called, which have been taken up and developed out of the Scriptures and become things with which people have become very much occupied, and in which they are very interested as things. So certain people hive off around a sanctification teaching, and they are the "sanctificationists", and it becomes an "ism." Others hive off; and they are bounded by the hedge of Second Adventism, the Lord's coming, prophecy, and all that. So you get groups like that. I want to say that would be utterly impossible if the Person of the Lord Jesus was dominant. What is the kingdom of God? It is Christ. If you get right inside of the Gospels you will find that the kingdom of God is Jesus Christ. If you are livingly in Christ, you are in the kingdom, and you know, as the Holy Spirit teaches you Christ, what the kingdom is in every detail. The kingdom is not some thing, in the first place. The kingdom, when it becomes something universal, will simply be the expression and manifestation of Christ. That is all. You come to the kingdom in and through Christ; and the same is true of everything else.

What is sanctification? It is not a doctrine. It is not an "it" at all. It is Christ. He is made unto us sanctification (1 Cor. 1:30). If you are in Christ and if the Holy Spirit is teaching you Christ, then you are knowing all about sanctification; and if He is not, you may have a theory and doctrine of sanctification, but it will separate you from other Christians, and it will be bringing any number of Christians into difficulties. Probably the teaching of sanctification as a thing has brought more Christians into difficulty than any other particular doctrine, through making it a thing, instead of keeping Christ as our sanctification.

I am only saying this to try to explain what I mean that it is in the School of Christ that we are to be found, where the Holy Spirit is not teaching us *things*; not Church doctrine, not sanctification, not adventism, not any *thing*, or any number of things, but teaching us Christ. What is adventism? What is the coming of the Lord? Well, it is the coming of the *Lord*. And what is the coming of the Lord? Well, such a word as this will give us the key: "He shall come to be glorified in His saints, and to be marvelled at in all them that believed" (2 Thess. 1:10). You see, it is the consummation of something that has been going on in an inward way. How then do I best know that the coming of the Lord draws nigh? Not best of all by prophetical signs, but by what is going on within the hearts of the Lord's people. That is the best sign of the times, namely, what the Spirit of God is doing in the people of God. But maybe you are not interested in that. You would far sooner know what is going to happen between Germany and Russia, whether these two eventually are going to become a great confederacy! How far does it get us? Where has all the talking about the revived Roman Empire got us? That is adventism as a thing. If only we keep close to Him who is the sum of all truth, and move with Him and learn Him, we shall know the course of things. We shall know what is imminent. We shall have in our heart whisperings of preparation. The best Advent preparation is to know the Lord. I am not saying that there is nothing in prophecy: don't misunderstand me. But I do know that there are multitudes of people who are simply engrossed in prophecy as a thing whose spiritual life counts for nothing, who really have no deep inward walk with the Lord. We have seen it so often.

I shall never forget on a visit to a certain country going into one of the big cities where I was to speak for a week. Everything was so arranged that my first message was timed to follow the last message of a man who had had a week before me, and he had been on prophecy for the whole week. I went into the last meeting where he gave his final message on the signs of the time. Notebooks were out, and they were taking it all down, fascinated. It was all external, all objective; such things as the Roman Empire revived and Palestine recovered. You know the sort of thing. Then he finished and they were waiting for some more, and the notebooks were ready. The Lord put it right into my heart that the first word was to be, "And every one that hath this hope set on him purifieth himself, even as he is pure" (1 John 3:3); to speak on the spiritual effect of that spiritual hope. They were not interested in that. The notebooks were closed, pencils put away, there was no interest as I sought in the Lord to be very faithful as to what all this should mean in an inward way, in adjustment to the Lord, and so on. They were only longing for the meeting to close. When I finished—they hardly waited for me to finish—they were up and out.

Oh no, it is the Lord, and the Holy Spirit would bring us back to the Lord, and it is not, after all, coming back to nonessentials, to elementary things, to come back to Christ. It is coming on to the only basis upon which the Holy Spirit can really accomplish all God's will and purpose, to be in the School of Christ where the Holy Spirit is teaching us Christ; and the Holy Spirit's way of teaching Christ is experimental.

The need of a new set of faculties

Now, here is where we become so seemingly elementary. You see, the very nature of this school requires the most drastic change in ourselves. It is impossible to get into the School of Christ, where the Holy Spirit is the great tutor, until the greatest change has taken place in us. We have to be made all over again or that school will mean nothing. We cannot come in here with any hope of learning Christ in the smallest way until a whole new set of faculties has been given to us. We have to have faculties given to us which we do not possess naturally. "Except one be born from above, he cannot see the kingdom of God" (John 3:3); and that is the Lord's way of stating a tremendous fact.

That kingdom is one in which certain things obtain with which I have no correspondence at all, with which naturally I have no power of communication. Take a walk round the garden. Walk down by the potatoes and vegetables and talk about, well, anything you like. What would the potatoes think about you? What would the cabbages say about you? They neither hear nor understand what you are talking about, whatever it is. Their kind of life is not your kind of life. They are not constituted in your kingdom. There is no correspondence between them and you at all. They have not the capacity, the gift, the qualification, for the most elementary things that you may be talking about. You may be talking about such foolish things as dress, ordinary everyday things: they do not know. It is like that. There is just as great a divide between us and the kingdom of God. "The natural man receiveth not the things of the Spirit of God: for they are foolishness unto him; and he cannot know them..." (1 Cor. 2:14). The divide is so utter that if you and I were brought in our natural state right into the place where the Spirit of God was speaking, unless that Spirit of God wrought a miracle in us, the whole thing would be of another world. And is it not so? You believers, go out into this world and talk about the things of the Lord and see men gape at you! It is all foreign to them. It is like that. "Except one be

born from above, he cannot see the kingdom of God."
To get into this school, something has to happen to us,
and that means that we have to be constituted anew, with
altogether other qualifications and abilities for the things
of God. That is the nature of this school. It is the School
of the Spirit of God.

I know that is very elementary, but, after all, is not that
the thing that is being pressed on us all the time? It is
being brought home to us how that we may hear words,
and yet that they may not mean anything to us. We need
our capacity for spiritual understanding enlarged more
and more. We are naturally handicapped in this whole
matter.

The breaking of the self-life

There is one passage that I cannot get away from. It has
been with me for a long time. It has been here as the basis
of our meditation. It is John 1:51, and it seems to me that
those are words which introduce us to the School of Christ,
namely, those words of the Lord Jesus to Nathanael. I
think it would be helpful to read the whole section from
verse 47:

*"Jesus saw Nathanael coming to him, and saith of him,
Behold, an Israelite indeed, in whom is no guile! Nathanael
saith unto him, Whence knowest thou me? Jesus answered
and said unto him, Before Philip called thee, when thou
wast under the fig tree, I saw thee. Nathanael answered
him, TEACHER, thou art the Son of God, thou art King of
Israel. Jesus answered and said unto him, Because I said
unto thee, I saw thee underneath the fig tree, believest
thou? thou shalt see greater things than these. And he
saith unto him, Verily, verily, I say unto you, Ye shall see*

*the heaven opened, and the angels of God ascending and
descending upon the Son of man."*

Here we are approaching the School of Christ, and there
is one thing which is essential before we can even come
to the threshold of that school, and that is what is marked
by those words, "Behold, an Israelite indeed, in whom
is no guile!" That put alongside the final words—"the
angels of God ascending and descending upon the Son of
man"—gives us a complete picture of what spiritually lies
behind.

At the time when Jacob in guile—you remember the
story of his guile—stole the birthright and had to escape
for his life, he saw a very great truth, though but dimly
as in type or figure, and a truth moreover into which he
was not then able to enter. Jacob at that time could never
have entered into the meaning of what he saw, namely,
the House of God, Bethel; that place where heaven and
earth meet, God and man meet, where the glory—uniting
heaven and earth, God and man—is the great link, where
God speaks and makes Himself known, where God's
purposes are revealed. Why was this the case with Jacob?
He was in guile. Let him leave it there then, as he must,
and go on, and for twenty years come under discipline,
and at the end of twenty years' discipline meet the impact
of heaven upon his earthly life, his earthly nature, the
impact of the Spirit upon his flesh, the impact of God
upon himself at Jabbok, and let that fleshly, natural life
be smitten and broken and withered, to bear the mark for
the rest of his days of its having come under the ban of
God; and then with the Jacob judged, the Jacob smitten,
wounded, withered, he can go back and pour out his drink-

offering at Bethel, and abide. The guile is dealt with. He is now not Jacob but Israel, in whom, speaking in type and figure, there is no guile. The work was not finished, but a crisis was met.

The Lord Jesus is saying here, to put it in a word, just this; to come into the place of the open heaven, where for you God is coming down in communication, and the glory of God abides, and where you enjoy what Bethel means, is nothing else than to come into Me; and to come into Me and abide in Me as the Bethel, the House of God, and have all the good of heaven and of God communicated, means you have come to the place where the natural life has been laid low, broken, withered. You cannot come into His school until that has happened, and it is necessary for the Lord to say to us in Christ as we come to the very threshold of that door, Behold, an Israelite indeed, in whom there is no Jacob; you shall see the heaven opened! To speak of the Jacob-life, is, after all, only another way of saying the self-life; for self is the very essence of the natural life; not just the self-life in its most positive evil forms, but the self-life in its totality. Jacob was in the elect line. He had a knowledge of God historically, but the transition from the natural to the spiritual was through discipline and crisis.

Let me stay with that. Here is the Lord Jesus. No one will dare to say that the self-life in Christ was like our self-life, polluted, corrupted, sinful. Not at all! And yet He had a self-life, a sinless self-life. For Him the self-life simply meant that He could act and speak and think and judge and move out from Himself. That is all. Not with evil intent, not as motivated or influenced by anything sinful or corrupt, but simply independently. He could have done and said a lot of good things independently. But He took the attitude, the position, that, although there was no sin in Him, He could not and would not at any time act or speak apart from His Father. That would be independence, and give the enemy just the opening that he was working for. But we can leave that.

My point is this, that you and I must not think of the self life only as something manifestly corrupt. There is a great deal done for God with the purest motive that is done out from ourselves. There are many thoughts, ideas, judgments, which are sublime, beautiful, but they are ours, and if we did but know the truth, they are altogether different from God's.

And so, right at the very door of His school the Lord puts something utter. It is Jabbok. Jabbok was a tributary of the Jordan, and the implications of Jordan are right there at the very threshold of the School of Christ. He accepted Jordan in order to enter into that school of the Spirit for three and a half years. You and I will not get into that school of the Anointing in any other way. It has to be like that. If you and I are going to learn Christ, it will only be as the Jacob-nature is smitten. I am not talking to you mere doctrine and technique. Believe me, I know exactly what I am talking about.

I know this thing as the greatest reality in my history. I know what it is to have been labouring with all my might for God and preaching the Gospel out from myself for years. Oh, I know; I know what hard labour it is with the dome over your head. How many times have I stood in the pulpit and in my heart have said, If only somehow or other I could get a cleavage through this dome over my head, and instead of preaching what I have gathered from books and put into my notebooks, and having to study it up, I could scrap the whole thing and, with an opened heaven, speak out what God is saying in my heart! That was a longing for years. I sensed there was something like this, but I had not got it until the great crisis of Romans 6 came, and with it the open heaven. It has been different ever since then, altogether different. "Ye shall see the heaven opened"; and all that strain has gone, all that bondage has gone, that limitation; there is no dome there. That is my glory today. Forgive that personal reference. I must say it, because we are not here to give addresses; we are right down on the reality of this matter of the Holy Ghost directly and immediately revealing Christ to us, and that ever-growingly; and this cannot be until we have come to our Jabbok, until the Jacob-life has been dealt with through that crisis, and the Lord is able to say, An Israelite indeed, in whom is no Jacob; thou shalt see heaven opened! There is that dome, that closed heaven over us by nature, but, blessed be God! the Cross rends the heavens, the veil is rent from top to bottom, and Christ is revealed through the rent veil of His flesh. He is no longer seen as the Man Jesus; He is seen in our hearts in all the fullness of God's consummate thought for man. It is a tremendous thing to see the Lord Jesus, and it is a tremendous thing to go on seeing Him more and more. That is where it begins— Behold, an Israelite indeed, in whom is no guile, no Jacob! Thou shalt see heaven opened!

A new prospect for a new man

That word, "thou shalt see heaven opened" is the new prospect for a new man. A new man, a new prospect! In the Authorized Version, a word is added which has been left out in the Revised Version. I take it for the simple reason that it is implicit in the original, without the word necessarily being introduced. In the Authorized it says, "Hereafter ye shall see heaven open." In the Revised Version, that first word is left out, and it simply reads, "Ye shall see...." But "ye shall" is something prospective, it is a tense pointing on to a future day. Not "ye are seeing", but "ye shall see." It is a new prospect for a new man; and therein lies a new era. It is the era of the Holy Spirit, for by the coming of the Holy Spirit, the open heaven is made a reality. The Cross effects the opening of the heavens for us, but it is the Holy Spirit who makes it good in us, just as was the case in that typical or symbolic death and burial and resurrection of the Lord Jesus in Jordan, when the heavens were opened to Him. Coming up on new, resurrection ground, He had the open heaven. The Spirit then alighted and abode upon Him, and the Spirit became, shall we say, the channel of communication, making the open heaven all that it should be as a matter of communication, intercourse, communion. It is the era of the Spirit, making all the values of Christ real in us. "Ye shall"; and, blessed be God, what was prospective for Nathanael is present for us.

That era has come. We are in the era of the Holy Spirit, of the open heaven.

The mark of a life anointed by the Holy Spirit

Now, what is, then, the mark of a life anointed by the Holy Spirit? You remember when Paul went to Ephesus, he found certain disciples and, without giving us any explanation of the reason for his question, he immediately said, "Did ye receive the Holy Spirit when ye believed?"

Their reply was, "We did not so much as hear whether the Holy Spirit was." Then Paul's next question is full of significance, taking us back to Jordan. "Into what then were ye baptized?" "Baptism is bound up with this vital reality. If you do not know the Holy Spirit, what can your baptism have meant?" Oh, we were baptized with John's baptism; Oh, I see: well, "John baptized with the baptism of repentance, saying unto the people, that they should believe on him that should come after him, that is, on Jesus." Then when they heard that, they were baptized into the Name of the Lord Jesus, they were baptized into Christ, and the Holy Spirit came upon them. Thus they came into the School of Christ; and the mark of a life anointed by the Spirit is that you know Christ in this living and ever-growing way.

Oh, listen to this, this is not so elementary and unnecessary as it may seem. Some of us, of course, are very poor scholars, and we take such a long time to learn. It took decades in my case to come to a true realization of this. We know so much, and we discover that our real personal knowledge of Christ is a poor thing. We are constantly brought up against that. At last, sooner or later, you and I are going to come to the place where we exclaim, "Oh, it is not doctrines and truths and themes and subjects and Scripture as mere matter that I need to know!" It is all very wonderful when you are taken up with it; but let a man come into the fires, into deep trial, into trouble and perplexity and then what about all your doctrines and all your themes, and all your Bible study? What is the value of it? It does not really solve your problem, it does not get you through. This is a tragedy. It is true of many of us who have got certain doctrines, who have gone through the doctrines of the Bible and worked them out, and who know what is in the Bible on these things; regeneration, redemption, atonement, righteousness by faith, sanctification, and so on; it is true that after we have gone through them all, and have got them all well worked out, and we come into a terrible spiritual experience, the whole thing counts for nothing, and we come to the place where, but for the Lord, we could easily throw the whole thing over and say, This Christianity does not work! Yes, for those who have known the Lord for years, so far as the accumulation of truth is concerned, that is about the value of it in an hour of the deepest spiritual distress. The only thing then that can help you is not your beautiful notebooks full of doctrines, but, What do I know of the Lord personally and livingly in my own heart? What has the Holy Spirit revealed in me and to me, and made a part of me, of Christ? Sooner or later, that is where we are coming to. We are going to be brought back to the living, spiritual knowledge of the Lord; for He alone personally, as revealed in our very being by the Holy Ghost, can save us in the deepest hour. The day will come when we will be stripped of everything but what is spiritually, inwardly known of Christ; stripped of all our mental and intellectual knowledge. Many of those who have been giants in teaching and in doctrine have had a very, very dark hour at the end of their lives, a very dark hour indeed. How they have got through has depended upon the inward knowledge of the Lord as over against mere intellectual knowledge. How can I explain what I mean by that?

Well, for example, you discover something in the realm

of food that really does help you. You have gone all round trying everything, all that the food people can provide to help you in a specific malady or weakness, and nothing has helped you. Then suddenly you discover something that really does help you, and the next time you are put to the test you take some of that and find you can go through on that. It is in you, something that gets you through your ordeal. That is what I mean, with reference to this question of how and what Christ is to be to us. He is to be in us, that upon which we can rest back in confidence and assurance, and, doing so, He gets us through. We are to know Him in that way. That is the only way in which to learn Christ, and that is experimental. "Ye shall see the heaven opened." The Holy Spirit has come to make for us an altogether new order of things, so that Christ is being revealed in us as our very life. Ye shall see when the Spirit comes: that is the mark of an anointed life. Ye shall see! And those are great moments when we do see. Some of us have had those great moments in specific connections, and some of us have seen others have their great moments in specific connections. Yet we have known that they knew all about the thing, and have been taught it, and have had it drummed into them for years; and then after years suddenly it has broken upon them, and they have said, Look here, I am now beginning to see what has been said all this time!

I remember a man brought up in a most saintly family, whose father I always used to liken to Charles G. Finney. He was like Charles G. Finney in spirit, soul and body; and one of his sons brought up in that most godly home was a great friend of mine for years. We had real fellowship together, always talking about the things of the Lord. One day—I can see it now right at the corner of Newington Green—I was going to meet him, and as I came toward Newington Green I saw him in the distance. I saw him smile, and we met and shook hands. He was one big smile. Do you know, I have made a discovery, he said. I said, What is your discovery? I have discovered that Christ is in me! "Christ in you, the hope of glory", has become a reality to me. Well, I said, I could have told you that years ago. Ah, that is the difference, he said: I see it now, I know it now.

You see what I mean. It is just that. Oh, that the world were full of Christians like that! Is this not the need? But inasmuch as this was said to Nathanael, it must be for us all. It was not said to Peter, James and John up on the Mount of Transfiguration: it was said to Nathanael, one of the general circle. It is for all; and if that wants strengthening, proving, notice what the Lord Jesus said—"Ye shall see the heaven opened, and the angels of God ascending and descending upon the Son of *man*." What has happened? A tremendous transition has taken place in the course of a few sentences. Behold, an Israelite indeed! That is for Israel; for Jacob, yes, the father of Israel; for sons of Jacob, the earthly Israel. Ah, yes, but that is purely within the limitation of earth, purely within the limitation of a people here amongst the nations, and within the limitation of types. Yes, but now for the tremendous transition. The Lord has cancelled out something Nathanael said. "Thou art King of Israel", said he. King of Israel? That is nothing. *Thou shalt see greater things than these. Thou shalt see the heaven opened, and the angels of God ascending and descending upon the Son of man!* That is something vastly greater than Israel. Son of Man! That is racial, that is universal; that is for all men who will come in, not just for Israel. Thou shalt see greater things! Heaven opened—and for whom? Not just for Israel, but for all men in Christ. The Son of Man!

That title, Son of Man, simply represents God's thought concerning man. Oh, the great, great thought and intention of God concerning man. The open heaven is for man when he comes into God's thought in Christ. The open heaven is for man: God revealing Himself to man in the Man. It is for all of us. Let no one think that this open heaven, this anointing, is for a certain few. Oh no, it is for everyone. God's desire, God's thought, is that you and I, the most simple, foolish, weak amongst men, the most limited naturally, with the least capacity naturally, should find that our very birthright is an open heaven. In other words, you and I may, in Christ, know this wonderful work of the Holy Spirit in an inward revelation of Christ in ever-growing fullness. That is for us, every one of us. May the most advanced Christian have a new movement toward the Lord in this matter, and all of us really come to this first crisis where the dome over us is cleft, and we know an open heaven, the Spirit revealing Christ in our hearts, for His glory.

7

Learning Under the Anointing

Reading: Matt. 11:29; John 1:51; Matt. 3:16; John 1:4;
Rom. 8:2; 2 Cor. 3:16-18.

The School of Christ; that is, the School where Christ
is the great Lesson and the Spirit the great Teacher; in the
School where the teaching is not objective but subjective,
where the teaching is not of things but an inward making
of Christ a part of us by experience—that is the nature of
this School.

The meaning of the anointing

"Ye shall see the heaven opened." "He saw the heavens
opened and the Spirit of God descending upon him."
What is the meaning of the anointing of the Holy Spirit.
It is nothing less and nothing other than the Holy Spirit
taking His place as absolute Lord. The anointing carries
with it the absolute lordship of the Holy Spirit, the Spirit
as Lord. That means that all other lordships have been
deposed and set aside; the lordship of our own lives; the
lordship of our own minds, our own wills, our own desires;
the lordship of others. The lordship of every interest and
every influence is regarded as having given place to the
undivided and unreserved lordship of the Holy Spirit, and

the anointing can never be known, enjoyed, unless that has taken place. That is why the Lord Jesus went down into Jordan's waters, into death and burial, in type, taking the place of man in representation, from that moment not to be under the government of His own life in any respect as He worked out the will of God, but to be wholly and utterly subject to the Spirit of God in every detail. Jordan's grave set forth the setting aside of every independent lordship, every other lordship, every other influence, and if you will read the spiritual life of Christ in the Gospels you will see that it was to that position that He was every moment adhering. Many and powerful were the influences which were brought to bear upon Him to affect Him and govern His movements. Sometimes it was the full force of Satan's open assault, to the effect that it was necessary that He should do certain things for His cause, or for His very continuance in life physically. Sometimes it was Satan clothing himself with the arguments and suasions of beloved associates, in their seeking to hold Him back from certain courses, or to influence Him to prolong His life by sparing Himself certain sufferings. In various ways influences were brought to bear upon Him from all directions, and many of the counsels were seemingly so wise and good. For example, with regard to His going up to the feast, it was urged, in effect: It is the thing that everybody is doing: if you do not go up you will prejudice your cause. If you really want to further this cause, you must fall into line with the accepted thing religiously, and you only stand to lose if you do not do that; you will curtail your influence, you will narrow your sphere of usefulness! And what an appeal that is if you have something very much at heart, some cause for God at heart, the success of which is of the greatest importance. Such then were the influences that were beating upon Him. But whether it be Satan coming in all the directness of his cunning, his wit, his insinuation, or whether it be through beloved and most intimate disciples and associates, whatever the kind of argument, that Man cannot be caused to deflect a hair's-breadth from His principle. "I am under the anointing; I am committed to the absolute sovereignty of the Holy Spirit, and I cannot move, whatever it costs. Cost it my life, cost it my influence, cost it my reputation, cost it everything that I hold dear, I cannot move unless I know from the Holy Spirit that that is the Father's mind and not another mind, the Father's will and not another will, that this thing comes from the Father." Thus He put back everything until He knew in His spirit what the Spirit of God witnessed. He lived up to this law, this principle, of the absolute authority, government, lordship of the anointing, and it was for that that the anointing had come.

That is the meaning of the anointing. Do you ask for the anointing of the Holy Spirit? Why do you ask for the anointing of the Holy Spirit? Is the anointing something that you crave? To what end? That you may be used, may have power, may have influence, may be able to do a lot of wonderful things? The first and pre-eminent thing the anointing means is that we can do nothing but what the anointing teaches and leads to do. The anointing takes everything out of our hands. The anointing takes charge of the reputation. The anointing takes charge of the very purpose of God. The anointing takes complete control of everything and all is from that moment in the hands of the

Holy Spirit, and we must remember that if we are going to learn Christ, that learning Christ is by the Holy Spirit's dealing with us, and that means that we have to go exactly the same way as Christ went in principle and in law.

So we find we are not far into the Gospel of John, which is particularly the Gospel of the spiritual School of Christ, before we hear even such as He saying, "The Son can do nothing of himself." "The words that I say unto you I speak not from myself." The works that I do are not Mine; "the Father abiding in me doeth his works."

"The Son can do nothing out from himself." You see, there is the negative side of the anointing; while the positive side can be summed up in one word—the Father only. Perhaps that is a little different idea of the anointing from what we have had. Oh, to be anointed of the Holy Spirit! What wonders will follow; how wonderful that life will be! The first and the abiding thing about the anointing is that we are imprisoned into the lordship of the Spirit of God, so that there can be nothing if He does not do it. Nothing! That is not a pleasant experience, if the natural life is strong and in any way in the ascendant. Therefore Jordan must be there before there can be an anointing. The putting aside of that natural strength and self-life is a necessity, for the anointing does carry with it essentially the absolute lordship of the Spirit.

You notice the issue of that in 2 Cor. 3:16. "When it shall turn to the Lord", when the Lord is the object in view, "the veil is taken away, and we all with unveiled face beholding as in a mirror the glory of the Lord are transformed into the same image... even as from the Lord the Spirit", or "the Spirit which is the Lord." You are in

the School and you can see Christ and learn Christ; which
is being transformed into the image of Christ under the
lordship of the Spirit. "When it shall turn to the Lord",
when the Lord is our object in view! But with us, with us
Christians, with us very devoted, very earnest Christians,
what a long time it takes to get the Lord as the sole object.
Is that saying a terrible thing? We say we love the Lord;
yes, but we do love to have our own way as well, and
we do not love to have our way thwarted. Have any of
us yet reached that point of spiritual attainment where
we never have a bad time at all with the Lord? Oh no,
we are still found at the place where we so often think it
is in the interests of the Lord that our hearts go out in a
certain direction, and the Lord does not let us do it, and
we have a bad time; and that has betrayed us absolutely.
Our hearts were in it. It was not easy, absolutely easy and
simple for us to say, Very well, Lord, I am just as pleased
as though you let me do it, I delight always to do Thy
will! We are disappointed the Lord does not let us do it;
or if the Lord delays it, what a time we go through. Oh,
if we could only get at it and do it! The time is finding
us out. Is that not true of most of us? Yes, it is true. We
do come into this picture, and that just does mean that,
after all, the Lord is not as verily our object as we thought
He was. We have another object alongside and associated
with the Lord; that is, something that we want to be or
to do, somewhere we want to go, something we want to
have. It is all there, and the Holy Spirit knows all about it.
In this School of Christ, where God's objective is Christ,
only Christ, utterly Christ, the very anointing means that
it has to be Christ as Lord by the Spirit. The anointing

takes that position. Well, so much for the moment for the meaning of the anointing. It was true in Him, and it has to be true in us.

"Lordship" and "subjection"

If we are going to graduate in this School, graduate to the glory, the ultimate full glory of Christ, to be the competent instrument in His Kingdom for government, the one way of learning that spiritual, Divine, heavenly government which is His destiny for the saints, is subjection to the Holy Spirit. That is a very interesting word, that word "subjection", in the New Testament. I think it has been rather mishandled and given a wrong and unpleasant meaning. The idea of subjection is usually that of being crushed down underneath, being put under all the time, suppression. "Wives, be in subjection to your own husbands." That is now interpreted as, You have to get down underneath; and the word does not mean that at all. How shall we seek to convey what the Greek word for subjection or submission really implies? Well, write down the number 1; and then you are going to write subjection or submission. How are you going to write it? Not by putting another 1 underneath. The word means "putting alongside it or after it." No. 1 is the primary number, it stands in front of all that comes after, and governs and gives value to all the rest. Subjection means that He in all things has the pre-eminence. We come after and take our value from Him. It is not being crushed down, but deriving everything from Him as the first one: and you never derive the benefits until you know subjection to Christ. That is to say, you come after, you take second place, take that place by which you derive all the benefit; you get the value by taking a certain place. The Church is not subject to Christ in that repressive sense, not down under His heel or His thumb, but just coming after, alongside, He having the pre-eminence, and the Church, His Bride, deriving all the good from His pre-eminence, from His having the first place. The Church second, yes; but who minds a second place if you are going to get all the values of the first by having second place? That is subjection. The Lord's idea for the Church is that she should have everything. But how will she get it? Not by taking the first place, but by coming alongside the Lord and in all things letting Him have the pre-eminence. That is submission, subjection. The lordship of the Spirit is not something hard that strips us, takes everything from us, and keeps us down there all the time so that we dare not move. The lordship of the Spirit is to bring us into all the fullness of that headship. But we do have to learn what that lordship is before we can come into that fullness. It is of His fullness we receive.

The trouble ever was, from Adam's day till ours, that it is not someone else's fullness that man wants, it is his own; to have it in himself and not in another. The Holy Spirit cuts that ground from under our feet and says, It is His fullness, it is in Him. He must have His place of absolute lordship before we can know of His fullness. That is enough I think, for the moment, on the meaning of the anointing. Do you grasp it? The Lord give us grace to accept the meaning of Jordan in order that we may have the open heaven and, by the open heaven, the anointing which brings in all heaven's fullness for us. But it does mean the absolute lordship of the Spirit. Lesson No. 1 in the School—oh, that is not Lesson No. 1, that is the very ground of coming into the School, that is a preliminary examination. We never get into the School until we accept the lordship of the Holy Spirit. That is why so many do not get on very far in the knowledge of the Lord. They have never accepted the implications of the anointing, never really come down into Jordan. Their progress, their learning, is very slow, very poor. Find a person who really knows the meaning of the Cross, of Jordan, in the clearing of the way for the lordship of the Spirit, and you will find quick growth, you will find spiritual development far ahead of all others. It is very true. That is the preliminary, the entrance examination.

The first lesson in the School of Christ

But when you are in, Lesson No. 1 begins here. It is but a reiteration of what has been strongly said in earlier meditations. The first lesson in the School of Christ which the Holy Spirit takes up to teach us is what we have called the altogether "other-ness" of Christ from ourselves. This may be not only the first lesson but a continuous lesson throughout life. But this is the one thing with which the Holy Spirit begins, the altogether "other-ness" of Christ from what we are. Will you take up the Gospel of John with that one thought in mind and read it again, quietly and steadily. How different Christ is from other people, even from His disciples. You can expand from John's Gospel to all the Gospels with that one thought. It will be an education to you if the Holy Spirit is with you as you read. How utterly different He is! That difference is again and again affirmed. "Ye are from beneath; I am from above" (John 8:23). That is a difference, and that difference becomes a clash all the way along; a clash of judgments, a clash of mentalities, a clash of minds, a clash of ideas, a clash of values; a clash in everything between Him and others, even with His disciples who are with Him in the School. His nature is different. He has a heavenly nature, a Divine nature. No one else has that. He has a heavenly mind, a heavenly mentality. They have an earthly mentality, and the two cannot meet, at any point. When the last word has been said, there is a big, big gap between the two. He is so utterly other.

Now, you say, that being so, we are at a very great disadvantage. He is one thing and we are another. But that is just the nature and meaning of this School. How is that problem going to be resolved? Well, it is just resolved like this, that He is all the time speaking about a time when He will be in them and they will be in Him, and when that time comes, in the innermost and deepest reality of their being, they will be altogether other than what they are in every other part of their being. That is to say, there will be in them that which is Christ, that which is Christ in all that He is as the absolutely Other. Sometimes they will think that the best thing to do is this, but that altogether Other inside will not let them do it. Sometimes they will think that the wise thing is not to do this, and that altogether Other inside keeps saying, in effect, Get on with it! The outer man says, It is madness! I am only courting disaster! The inner Man says, You are to do it! These two cannot be reconciled. He is within and He is altogether other, and our education is to learn to follow Him, to go His way. "If any man will come after me, let him deny himself... and follow me." Deny himself: your arguments, your judgments, your common sense sometimes. Follow

Me!—and Christ is vindicated every time. Men have done the maddest things from this world's standpoint and have been vindicated. This is no suggestion that you should go and begin to do mad things. I am talking about the authority of Christ within, the difference of Christ from ourselves, and this is the first lesson the Holy Spirit would teach anyone coming into the School of Christ, that there is this great difference, this great cleavage, that He is one thing and we are quite another; and we can never be sure that we are on the right line save as we submit everything to Him.

This is why prayer has to have such a large place in the life of a child of God, and this is why prayer had such a large place in His life when He was here. The prayer life of the Lord Jesus is, in a certain realm and sense, the biggest problem that you can face. He is Christ, He is the Son of God, He is under the anointing of the Holy Spirit, and He is without sin in His person, and yet, and yet, He must spend all the night in prayer after a heavy and long day's work. Again and again you come upon Him in prayer. Why must He pray? Because there are other influences at work, there are other things which are seeking to call for consideration and response and obedience, and He must keep all the time in line with the anointing, in harmony with the Spirit under whose government He has placed Himself, because He can decide nothing out from Himself. If He must do that, what of us? We are not even on His sinless level. We have all that in our very natures which works violently against God, God's mind, God's will. How much the more necessary then is it for us to have a prayer life, by which the Spirit is given an opportunity of keeping us straight, keeping us on the line of Divine purpose, keeping us in the ways of the Lord, and in the times of the Lord.

Beloved, if there is one thing that a child of God will learn under the Holy Spirit's lordship, it is this thing, namely, how different He is from us, how different we are from Him, how altogether other. But, blessed be God, now in this dispensation, if we are truly children of God, the altogether Other is not merely objective but within. That is the second phase of this matter of the "other-ness." The first phase is the fact of the difference. Will you accept this? Will you now, at this very point, this moment, just settle this? The Lord Jesus is altogether other than I am: even when I think I am most perfectly right, He may still be altogether other, and I can never, never rely upon my own sense of rightness until I have submitted my rightness to Him! That is very utter, but it is very necessary. Many of us have learned these lessons. We are not talking out of a book, we are talking out of our own experience. We have been quite sure at times that we were right and we have gone forward to follow out our rightness in that judgment, and we have come to grief, and we have got into an awful fog of perplexity and bewilderment. We were quite sure we were right, but look where we have been landed! And when we come to think about it, and put it before the Lord, we have to ask ourselves, how much did I wait on the Lord and wait for the Lord about that thing. Were we not a bit precipitate with our own sense of rightness? And that is David and the ark all over again. David's motive was all right and David's sense of God's purpose was all right. That God wanted the ark in Jerusalem was right enough, but David got the thing into his soul as an idea, and it worked itself up as a great enthusiasm within him, and so he made the cart. The motive, the good motive, the good idea, the devout spirit, got him into most awful trouble. The Lord smote Uzzah, and he died before the Lord, and the ark went into the house of Obededom, and tarried there, all because man had a good and right idea, but had not waited on the Lord. You know the sequel. Later on, David said to the heads of the Levites, "Sanctify yourselves, both ye and your brethren, that ye may bring up the ark of the Lord, the God of Israel, unto the place that I have prepared for it. For because ye bare it not at the first, the Lord our God made a breach upon us, for that we sought him not according to the ordinance." The instruction was there all the time, but he had not waited on the Lord. If David had brought his devout enthusiasm quietly before the Lord, He would have directed him to the instruction He had given to Moses, and said, in effect, "Yes, all right, but, remember, this is how it is to be carried." There would have been no death, no delay, things would have gone right through.

Yes, we may get a very good idea for the Lord, but we have to submit it to the Lord, to be quite sure it is not our idea for the Lord, but the Lord's mind being born in us. It is very important to learn Christ; He is so other.

You see, this divides Christians very largely into two classes. Christians can be, in the main, divided into these two classes. There is that very large class of Christians whose Christianity is objective, is outward. It is a matter of having adopted a Christian life, that now they do a lot of things which they once would not do. They go to meetings, they go to church, they read the Bible, lots of things that they used not to do; and they now do not do quite a lot of things they once did. That is what holds good more or less in that class. It is now a matter of not doing and doing, not going and going, being a good Christian outwardly. That is a big class with its various degrees of light and shade, a very big class of Christians indeed.

There are others who are in this School of Christ, for whom the Christian life is an inward thing of walking with the Lord and knowing the Lord in the heart, in greater or lesser degree. That is the nature of it, a real inward walk with a living Lord in their own heart. There is a great deal of difference between those two classes.

The Spirit's law or instrument of instruction

Well now, I must come to a close. The altogether "other-ness"; by what means does the Spirit make that "other-ness" known to us?—for the Spirit does not speak to us in audible language and words. We do not hear an outside voice saying, This is the way, walk ye in it! Then how are we to know? Well, it is in what the Apostle Paul calls "the law of the Spirit of life in Christ Jesus." "In him was life; and the life was the light." How are we to know, by what means are we to be enlightened on this matter, on the difference between our ways, our thoughts, our feelings, and the Lord's? How are we to have light? The life was the light. "He that followeth me shall not walk in the darkness, but shall have the light of life" (John 8:12). "The law of the Spirit of life in Christ Jesus made me free from the law of sin and of death." Then the Spirit's instrument, if I may call it that, of our education is life in Christ. That is to say, we know the mind of the Spirit on matters by quickening, by sensing, discerning life, Divine life, the Spirit of life. Or, on the other hand, if we are alive to the Lord, we know when the Spirit is not in agreement with anything by a sense of death, death in that direction.

That is the thing that no one can teach us by words, by giving us a lesson. But it is a thing we can know. You know it by reactions, violent reactions often. You have taken a course, and you get a bad reaction. You strive in a certain direction to realize a certain thing, and if only you would stop for a moment and look at it, you know that you are trying to bring that about. You know quite well that this thing is not spontaneous, that this lacks the spontaneity which is a mark of the Lord. You know the Lord is not coming through there. You know quite well that you have no sense of spontaneity and peace. It has to be forced, to be driven, to be made to happen. More or less, I think, every one of you who is a true child of God knows what I am talking about. But remember, this is the Spirit's instrument in the School for teaching Christ—life. The mark of a Spirit-governed, Spirit-anointed, man or woman is that they move in life, and that they minister life, and that what comes from them means life, and they know by that very law of life where the Lord is, what the Lord is in, what the Lord is after, what the Lord wants. That is how they know. No voice is heard, no objective vision is seen, but deep in the spirit life arbitrates, the Spirit of life.

How necessary it is for us to be alive unto God in Christ Jesus. How necessary it is for us to be all the time laying hold on life. If Satan can only bring his spirits of death to bear upon us and bring our spirit under the wrappings of death, he will cut off the light at once and leave us floundering; we do not know where we are, what to do. He is always seeking to do that, and ours is a continuous battle for life. Everything for the realization of God's purpose is bound up with this "life." This "life" is potentially the sum of all Divine purpose. Just as in the seed there is the life, not only of the seed, but of a great tree, and that life, if but released, will eventuate in that great tree, so in the life given to us in our spiritual infancy, our new birth, there is all the power of God's full and final and consummate thought, and Satan is out, not just to cut off our life, but to prevent God's final interests and concerns in the full display which is in that life which is given to us, that eternal life given to us now. The Spirit is always concerned with that life, and He would say to us, Guard that life: do not allow anything to come to interfere with that life: see that whenever there is something that grieves the Spirit and arrests the operation of that life, you immediately resort to the precious Blood which stands as a witness against all the death, that precious Blood of Jesus, the incorruptible life, the witness in heaven to victory over sin and death, by which you can be delivered from that arresting hand of Satan. That precious Blood is the ground upon which we must stand to deal with everything that grieves the Spirit and checks the operation of life, by which we come to know, and know in this living way, Christ in ever-growing fullness. The Lord help us.

8

The Governing Law of Divine Love

Reading: John 1:4; 2:3; 3:3; 4:13-14; 5:5-9; 6:33-35; 9:1-7; 11:1-6, 17, 21, 23, 25-26.

A zero point

All these passages which we have read are really a sequence. They are the outflow of the first. "In him was life; and the life was the light of men." And you will notice that they all represent a zero point. The mother of Jesus said unto Him, They have no wine: there is nothing to draw upon! The next chapter is only another way of saying the same thing. Nicodemus came to Jesus and sought to commence at a point which he considered to be a good point from which to begin negotiations with the Lord Jesus, but it was a point far in advance of that which the Lord Jesus could accept: so He took him right back to zero, and said: Ye must be born again. We cannot start at any point beyond that. If you and I are going to come into any kind of living relationship, we must get right back there: we must come to zero and start from zero. "Ye must be born again." For except a man be born anew, he cannot see. It is no use our starting at some point where, after all, we are incapacitated from seeing. Chapter 4 is but another way of setting forth the same truth. The woman after all is found to be bankrupt, at zero. Jesus gradually draws her out and the final expression from her side is, in effect, Well, I don't know anything about that, I have not anything of that; I have been coming here every day, day after day, but I know nothing about what you are talking of! She is down to zero: and then He says, That is where we begin. The water that I shall give is not the drawing upon your own resources at all, not bringing something out of your well, it is not something that you can produce and I improve upon and make better. No, it is something which comes solely and only from Myself; it is a new act altogether apart from you; it is the water that I shall give. We begin all over again in this matter.

Then in chapter 5 the Holy Spirit is careful to make perfectly clear that this poor fellow was in a hopeless state, that every effort was abortive, every hope was disappointed. For thirty and eight years, a lifetime, the man had been in that state, and there is the note of despair in the man. The Lord Jesus does not say to him, Look here, you are a poor cripple; I am going to take you in hand, and after a course of treatment I will have you on your feet, I will make those old limbs over anew, I will improve on your condition. Not at all. In an instant, in a moment, it is a start again. The effect of what He does is as though the man were born again. This is not curing the old man, this is making a new man, in principle. This is something that comes in that was not there before, and could not be produced before, the ground of which was not there, something which was uniquely and solely Christ's doing. It was zero, and He began at zero.

Chapter 6—a great multitude. Whence shall we buy bread enough for this multitude? Well, the situation is quite a hopeless one, but by His own act He meets the situation, and then follows on with His great teaching to interpret what He has done in feeding the multitude. He says, I am the Bread which came down from heaven. There is nothing here on this earth that can meet this need; it has to come out of heaven, Bread out of heaven for the life of the world: otherwise the world is dead. We begin at zero. (The loaves and fishes may represent our small measure of Christ which can be increased.)

Chapter 9—the man born blind. Not a man who has lost his sight and is having his sight recovered. That is not the point at all. The glory of God is not found in improving, the glory of God is found in resurrection. That is what is coming out here. The glory of God is not found in our being able to produce something or put something into God's hands, something of ours, that He can take up and make use of. The glory of God is something solely out from God Himself, and we can contribute nothing. The glory of God comes out of zero. The man was born blind. The Lord Jesus gives him sight; he never had sight before.

Then chapter 11 gathers it all up. If you like to sit down and look at Lazarus, you will find that Lazarus is the embodiment of "They have no wine." He is the embodiment of "Ye must be born again." He is the embodiment of "the water that I shall give shall be in him...." He is the embodiment of a bankrupt state; in the grave four days; but the Lord is coming to that. Lazarus is the embodiment of chapter 6: "I am the living bread which came down out of heaven... for the life of the world." Lazarus is the embodiment of chapter 9, a man who is without sight, who is given sight by the Lord Jesus. Lazarus gathers it all up. But if you notice, in gathering up everything, the Holy Spirit is very careful to stress and emphasize one thing, namely, that the Lord Jesus will not touch the thing until it is far, far removed from any human remedy. He will not come on to the scene, or into association with it, until from all human standpoints it is bankrupt, it is at zero. And this is not a question of lack of interest, lack of sympathy, or lack of love, for here the Spirit again points out that love was there. But love is bound by a law.

The governing law—the glory of God

Divine love is bound by a law. Love has a law where God is concerned. God's love is under a law. God's love is under the law of the glory of God, and He can show His love only in so far as showing His love is going to be to His glory. He is governed by that. In all the showings of His love, His object is that He may be glorified, and the glory of God is bound up with resurrection. "Said I not unto thee, that if thou wouldest believe, thou shouldest see the glory of God?" "Thy brother shall rise again." The glory of God is in resurrection, and therefore love demands that everything shall come to the place where only resurrection will meet the situation; no curing of things, no remedying of the old man.

Oh, let me start right back at the beginning if it is necessary. There are still a lot of people in this world who think that there is something in man that can contribute to the glory of God and that Christianity is only the bringing up out of man of something that is for the glory of God.

That is a long-, long-standing fallacy and lie. It is not true. Call it what you like; it goes by various names, such as "the inner light" or "the vital spark." The Word of God all the way through is coming down tremendously on this thing. I start at zero, and zero for me means that I can contribute nothing. Everything has to come from God. The very fact that the gift of God is eternal life means that you have not got it until it is given to you. You are blind until God gives you the faculty of sight. You are dead until God gives you life. You are a hopeless cripple until God does something for you and in you which you can never do. Unless God does this thing, unless this act takes place, well, there you lie. Spiritually, that is how you are. You can contribute nothing. Nicodemus, you have nothing to give, you must be born again; I cannot take you at the point at which you come to Me! Woman of Samaria, you have nothing, and you know it and confess it: that is where I begin! Man of Bethesda, you can do nothing, and you know it: then it all rests with Me! If ever there is to be anything, it rests with Me! Lazarus, what can you do now, and what can anybody make of you? If I do not come right in as out from heaven and do this thing, then there is nothing but corruption!

This is one of the great lessons that you and I have to learn in the School of Christ, that God begins for His glory at zero, and God will take pains through the Holy Spirit to make us to know that it is zero; that is, to bring us consciously to zero, and make us realize it is all with Him. You see, the end is always governing God, and the end is His glory. Take that word through this Gospel again—the glory of God in relation to Christ. We were saying in a previous meditation that God's great end for us in Christ is glory, fullness of glory. Yes, but then there is this—that no flesh should glory before Him. And where does that come?—"He that glorieth, let him glory in the Lord" (1 Cor. 1:29-31). And what is that connected with?—He "was made unto us wisdom from God, and righteousness and sanctification, and redemption: that, according as it is written, He that glorieth, let him glory in the Lord." It is a question of what He is made to be. No flesh is to glory before Him. "My glory will I not give to another" (Isa. 42:8; 48:11). Therefore it is all the Lord's matter and He will retain it in His own hands. "And when he had heard... he abode two days... where he was" (John 11:6). In love, governed by love, that the glory of God might be revealed, He kept away.

Have we got settled on this? We take so long to learn these basic elementary lessons. We do still cling to some sort of idea that we can produce something, and all our miserable days are simply the result of still hoping that we can in some way provide the Lord with something. Not being able to find it, but breaking down all the time, we get miserable, perfectly miserable. It takes us so long to come to the place where we do fully and finally settle this matter, that if we lived as long as ever man lived on this earth, we shall not be able to contribute one iota which can be acceptable to God, and which He can take and use for our salvation, for our sanctification, for our glorification, not a bit. All that He can use is His Son, and the measure of our ultimate glory will be the measure of Christ in us, just that. There will be differences in glory, as one thing differs from another. One glory of the sun, another of

the moon, another of the stars. There will be differences
in degree of glory, and the difference in degree of glory
ultimately will be according to the measure of Christ that
each one of us severally has. That in turn depends upon
how much you and I by faith are really making Christ the
basis of our life, the very basis of our living, of our being,
how much the principle of these familiar words has its
application in our case, "Not what I am, but what Thou
art." Christ is all the glory, "the Lamb is all the glory in
Immanuel's land."

Beloved friends, whatever you go away with, go
away with this, that from God's standpoint, the glory
of life depends entirely upon our faith apprehension,
appropriation and appreciation of Christ, and there is no
glory at all for us now or in the time to come but on that
ground and on that line. I know how simple that is, how
elementary, but oh, it is such a governing thing. Glory—
that the Lord shall be glorified in us. What greater thing
could happen than that the Lord should be glorified in us?
The glory of God is bound up with the resurrection, and
resurrection is God's unique and sole prerogative. So that
if God is to be glorified in us, you and I have to live on
Him as the resurrection and the life from day to day, and
know Him as that as we go through life.

RHP Essential Classics

T. AUSTIN-SPARKS
   The School of Christ
   The inner working of the Holy Spirit

JOHN BUNYAN
   The Pilgrim's Progress
   The classic allegory of the Christian life

CHARLES FINNEY
   Revival
   God's way of revival

ROY HESSION
   The Calvary Road
   The way of personal revival
   We Would See Jesus
   Seeing in Jesus everything we need
   The Power of God's Grace
   The way of peace, joy and genuine revival
   When I Saw Him
   Renewing your vision of Jesus
   Our Nearest Kinsman
   *The message of revival, restoration and redemption
      from the book of Ruth*

Please ask for these titles at your local
Christian bookshop

RHP Essential Classics

ANDREW MURRAY
  The True Vine
  Fruitfulness and stability in Jesus
  The Full Blessing of Pentecost
  Power from on High

OSWALD J. SMITH
  The Revival We Need
  A heart-stirring cry for revival
  The Enduement of Power
  Being filled with the Holy Spirit

R. A. TORREY
  How to Study the Bible
  Profit and pleasure from the Word of God
  How to Pray
  Praying with power and authority

DAVID WILKERSON
  Hungry For More of Jesus
  The way of intimacy with Christ
  Hallowed Be Thy Names
  Knowing God through His names

For information about our full range of books, please visit our website at **www.rhpbooks.co.uk** or send a medium-sized stamped addressed envelope to RHP, PO Box 576, Aylesbury, HP22 6XX.